William J Fay

P9-CZV-111

# GOOD NEWS STUDIES

Volume 11

# Leadership in Paul

*by*

*Helen Doohan*

Michael Glazier, Inc.

Wilmington, Delaware

## ABOUT THE AUTHOR

Helen Doohan is Assistant Professor of Religious Studies and Director of the CREDO Program at Gonzaga University. Her articles have been published in Biblical Theology Bulletin, Review for Religious and Journal of Religion and Health. She travels extensively, lecturing and offering workshops throughout the U.S., Canada, Australia and New Zealand. Her academic interests include biblical theology and leadership.

First published in 1984 by Michael Glazier, Inc.
1723 Delaware Avenue, Wilmington, Delaware 19806

©1984 by Michael Glazier, Inc. All rights reserved.

**Library of Congress Cataloging in Publication Data**

Doohan, Helen
    Leadership in Paul.
    (Good news studies; v. 11)
    Bibliography: p. 197
    1. Christian leadership—Biblical teaching.
    2. Bible. N.T. Epistles of Paul—Criticism, interpretation, etc.
    3. Christian leadership—Bibliography.
I. Title.
II. Series
BS2655.L42D66     1984     262'.1     84-81249
ISBN 0-89453-435-1

The Bible text in this publication is from the Revised Standard Version of the Bible, copyrighted 1946, 1952, ©1971, 1973 by the Division of Christian Education of the National Council of the Churches of Christ in the U.S.A., and used by permission.

Typography by Rick Huber
Printed in the United States of America

*I gratefully dedicate this
book to Leonard, my husband,
friend and colleague.*

# Acknowledgements

I would like to express my appreciation and gratitude to Dr. Ronald R. Kelly, Father Patrick J. Ford, S.J. and Father Charles D. Skok for their careful reading of the manuscript and helpful comments and suggestions; to Father Wilfrid Harrington, O.P. for his assistance in the later stages of editing, and to Mrs. Darlene Mitchell for her diligent preparation of sections of the text.

I extend very special thanks to my family, Leonard and Eve-Anne, for their loving support and encouragement.

# CONTENTS

# INTRODUCTION

# THE ESSENTIALS OF CHRISTIAN LEADERSHIP

Among the more important critical issues of this decade is the crisis of leadership in society and in the church. Although many studies and analyses are available on the issue, the crisis continues to persist.[1] Questions are raised regarding leaders and leadership. Those who exercise leadership in any given group are becoming cautious and hesitant because of a prevailing attitude of criticism and confrontation. Among religious leaders, the issue increases in delicacy and complexity because tradition and commitment are also involved. The focus of this study is Christian leadership, but the sources and insights will encompass both the secular and the religious spheres.[2] After briefly reflecting

---

[1]Notable studies include those of Stogdill, *Handbook of Leadership*, a compilation of leadership research, theory and process; Burns, *Leadership*, an exploration and analysis of various types of leadership in well known historical figures; Schillebeeckx, *Ministry: Leadership in the Community of Jesus Christ*, a historical perspective of leadership in the church from New Testament times to the present; Hersey and Blanchard, *Management of Organizational Behavior*, a synthesis and a projection of leadership styles in and for our time.

[2]Since the Second Vatican Council urges the church to see itself in the world and at the service of the world, these dual sources are appropriate. See the documents on *The Church, The Church in the Modern World*, and *The Laity* in particular.

on the crisis in the church, this chapter addresses the general issues of leadership theory, as well as the distinctive component of religious leadership. The method and approaches to the study are outlined and terms defined. Because of the origins of Christianity, a selection of first century religious influences is examined. Finally, a perspective on the early Christian leader, Paul, is offered to enable the reader to focus on the specifics of this research. In addition, a description of terms under the broad categories of authority, power and leadership is in the appendix for convenient reference.

## The Crisis in the Church

Within the Christian church in general and the Catholic church in particular, there is a situation comparable to that of contemporary society, a prevailing apprehension and mistrust, alongside a paucity of viable models of leadership.[3] The changes in roles and emphases since the Second Vatican Council have created an urgent need for a new kind of leadership. Priests and laity are examining their responsibilities and their inter-relationships. The role of women in ministry is undergoing radical change. Likewise, the problem of burnout among committed leaders and the demands made on innovative and dynamic leaders are contributing to the crisis.[4] Furthermore, whoever assumes a leadership role today must have the potential of taking creative steps in

---

[3]See Maccoby, *The Leader*, pp. 17-21, where the author presents the theses of his study. "The first, simply stated, is that a new model of leadership is needed to bring out the best, not only in a new social character, but also in the older social characters that coexist with it. To determine what kind of leader we need, we must also understand how we are changing and why old models of leadership no longer serve" (17). "The second thesis...is that in any organizational society good leadership at the top is not enough" (21). There are obvious parallels to the Catholic Church today.

[4]See H. Doohan, "Burnout: a Critical Issue for the 1980's" for a synthesis of this contemporary phenomenon and some possible solutions. Haring, p. 110,notes that "immobile, regressive church leaders enjoy a longer life span than dynamic leaders."

dealing with a diversity of new situations and demands. The crisis of leadership is closely related to the crisis of authority. Many speak of the decline in authority and the need for change in structures and in attitudes. Tensions exist because of leadership preferences within the faith community and long-standing institutional structures. Freedom, power, responsibility, mutual respect, and charism are among the terms utilized in the discussion of authority in the church. Biblical as well as contemporary perspectives are being examined for insights into the question of authority. However, authority must be conceived of differently in a pluralistic church where being an individual and being part of a community are equally emphasized values. The situation is not unlike that of the New Testament community, with a similar co-operation and co-responsibility being necessary today. Among the demands in a pluralistic church are the ability to live with complexity and ambiguity and the ability to deal with conflict. Haring suggests that a training for genuine constructive criticism is essential in a pluralistic and dynamic world.[5] An aspect of the crisis in the church today is this inability to criticize ideas and positions rather than people. Furthermore, this critical skill will continue to grow in importance as the church continues in crisis and therefore calls for a unique kind of leadership.

Implied in the assessment of the crisis in the church is the need for a new way of approaching followership. In addition to the usual tensions implied in any dynamic relationship is the religious conviction within the church that both leaders and followers are equally inspired by the Spirit. The quality of listening and the degree of authentic communication this reality demands is a continuous challenge for persons in the Christian community. Mutual confidence and respect are the perennial qualities necessary in all persons who presume to interact effectively. These qualities must be developed as the crisis anticipates changes in orientation and thinking.

[5]See Haring, p. 114.

The contemporary church is called upon to adapt to changing needs within the Christian community. In this regard, the education of leaders and potential leaders is a prime concern. Their training must include an ability to respond creatively in an ever changing world. It will also mean a more integrated and wholistic approach to personal development and to human life. Finally, among the essential qualities of leaders will be flexibility, an attitude of service and caring, and the willingness to share power and responsibility. Within the Christian community is a specific call for an understanding of church, of persons and gifts, of scripture and of Christ, which will sensitize leaders and followers to the demands and the challenges of this age, and an appropriate Christian response. The crisis in the church can lead to a courageous step into the future if rightly approached. However, the vision of, and for, the future ought to be shared by all persons in the faith community. The task then, is both urgent and crucial if the church is to continue to exist.

## *Leadership — A Perspective*

In the study of leadership, a number of interesting theories have emerged and been analysed.[6] While some look for greatness of character and person to account for leadership ability, others stress the relationship of leadership to structure, to goals and to motivation. Under discussion are the contingency theories that see leadership effectiveness based on situational demands. In fact, work-oriented or interaction-oriented leaders are effective in different situations. The characteristics of any given leader and the demands of the situation seem to give rise to certain individ-

[6]Among some of the theories are the following in Stogdill, pp. 17-22: Great Man theories, Environmental theories, Personal-Situational theories, Interaction-Expectation theories, Humanistic theories and Exchange theories. Numerous studies constitute the empirical evidence for the findings and categorization. Hollander, in "What is the Crisis of Leadership," synthesizes these early theories in a readable fashion.

uals as leaders. However, some studies have indicated a favored or specific approach to the exercise of leadership. A good example is McGregor's theory 'X' and theory 'Y' which has since been modified by others.[7] Role differentiation has also been examined in order to understand the dynamics of leadership. It would seem that leadership is a dynamic process that changes and varies in response to situational changes. If this analysis is correct, then leadership behavior, rather than leadership traits is more important for one's understanding of this phenomenon. Furthermore, certain situations are more favorable for leaders to exercise influence over a group.

Another insight is offered by Volleberg who considers an integrated approach to leadership.[8] While gifted people need the space and the possibility of using their talents, group needs must also be kept in mind. Because of these two factors and their interrelatedness, the leader in such a situation can discover himself/herself functioning in the midst of tension. When James McGregor Burns assesses moral leadership, he suggests that accepting conflict, being unloved

[7]See Hersey and Blanchard, p. 49, for a synthesis of the theory as well as for modifications and developments. A chart summarizes the major points:
Theory X:
1. Work is inherently distasteful to most people.
2. Most people are not ambitious, have little desire for responsibility, and prefer to be directed.
3. Most people have little capacity for creativity in solving organizational problems.
4. Motivation occurs only at the physiological and safety levels.
5. Most people must be closely controlled and often coerced to achieve organizational objectives.
Theory Y:
1. Work is as natural as play, if the conditions are favorable.
2. Self-control is often indispensable in achieving organizational goals.
3. The capacity for creativity in solving organizational problems is widely distributed in the population.
4. Motivation occurs at the social, esteem, and self-actualization levels, as well as physiological and security levels.
5. People can be self-directed and creative at work if properly motivated.

[8]See Volleberg, p. 48, who calls integrated leadership an approach which combines autonomous leadership and the activity of the group. This approach often of necessity deals with tension and conflict.

and the acceptance of the reality that no group is totally harmonious are some of the prerequisites for this type of transforming leadership.[9] Furthermore, two levels of consciousness are demanded of leaders according to Greenleaf. One level is totally in touch with the real world; the other is detached enough to perceive the sweep of history and the future possibilities hidden from others.[10] The attitude of a servant is essential for the acceptance of this kind of leadership. While leadership theories offer a perspective, the constitutive aspects of leadership also need to be examined and assessed. Among these constitutive aspects are the characteristics and functions of the leader as well as an understanding of the followers or group.

Although the characteristics of leadership may be culturally conditioned, and acceptable attitudes in leaders may be determined by the situation, some statements about leaders can be made. For example, leaders tend to be persons who emanate confidence and self-assurance. There is also a high correlation between leadership and originality, sociability, aggressiveness, judgment, desire to excel, cooperativeness, humor, and liveliness. Little correlation seems to exist between physique, energy, age or appearance and leadership. However, recent literature seems to emphasize self-acceptance and self-awareness as related to leadership style. Persons who understand and accept themselves, their needs and weaknesses tend to be more effective leaders and decision makers. In fact, acceptance of various dimensions of personality is far more important than "perfection."[11] High self-esteem seems to be important in crisis situations, when the leader is under stress, and in circumstances where

---

[9] See Burns, chapter 2, on the "Structures of Moral Leadership." and Appendix, pp. 206-207 for descriptions of leadership styles.

[10] See Greenleaf, *Servant Leadership*, p. 26.

[11] Hamachek, p. 359, states: "...persons in leadership positions who have made their peace with their occasional failures and unreached goals will probably be better leaders because they have learned that to be fully human is to be fully fallible."

the desires and support of followers is variable and shifting.[12]

There are many ways of understanding the functions of leadership.[13] In some instances, the effectiveness of certain types of leaders is related to their ability and judgment in understanding motivation and in working through and with people. However, some approaches have obvious drawbacks, and the authoritarian personality or tendency in leadership is such an example. Often negative factors such as fear of isolation and a sense of powerlessness determine this approach. It would appear that authoritarianism is a way of stifling the group achievement of goals and the individual's satisfaction of needs except on a very primitive level. An authoritarian attitude utilizes power in a coercive or manipulative manner rather than in a persuasive way. Tasks may be completed by leaders functioning in this mode, but the development of persons and groups remains in an early dependent stage. Rather, the leader who sees his or her role as service of others will bring other more creative dynamics into operation.

Other functions of leadership include serving the dreams and aspirations of others, allowing the group as well as the leader to articulate the dream, exerting a prophetic influence in time of crisis, or exercising a charismatic influence in a vital aspect of life. These ways of functioning as a leader are open to input from the group and are responsive to the uniqueness of the situation. While these functions are not

[12]Hamachek, p. 358, suggests these tentative conclusions: "1. A high self-esteem leader may hold up better in a crisis and under stress because of a more stable self-image, which is, in fact, reflected in high self-esteem; 2. A high self-esteem leader is less apt to be unduly swayed by the shifting and sometimes whimsical moods of public opinion and in that sense he may be more dependable and predictable; 3. High self-esteem is a sign that a person likes himself, which may be a fairly good indicator of how he may be inclined to feel about others."

[13]See Appendix pp 202-205 for descriptions of authority and power; also Stogdill, p. 26: "Harding (1949) proposed 21 types of educational leadership as follows: autocrat, cooperator, elder statesman, eager beaver, pontifical, muddled, loyal staff man, prophet, scientist, mystic, dogmatist, open-minded, philosopher, business expert, benevolent despot, child protector, laizzez-faire, community-minded, cynic, optimist, and democrat."

exhaustive, they provide a perspective that will be developed in this study.

In order to function as a leader, an awareness of the group's purpose or goal is paramount. Groups can be described as task or maintenance oriented, primary or secondary, affective, emotionally toned or functional. Groups require a leadership response consistent with their purpose or goals. In fact, if expectations, such as personal growth, are not realized, then leadership is perceived as ineffective. Another variable to be considered is the maturity of the followers in a given sphere. The level of maturity often requires a particular leadership approach. Other distinctions such as group cohesiveness, and natural or experimental groupings, affect the dynamics of leadership as does authoritarianism among followers.[14] A leader must be cognizant of the potential and the weakness in the various situations, for leadership today requires a cooperation and responsiveness rather than a passivity. Generally, shared responsibility and some delegation of authority contribute to group effectiveness. Leadership seems to comprise interaction, participation and a working relationship with followers and within the group. Hollander even suggests that since "leadership depends upon responsive followership, followers may justifiably feel that they have a vital role in the process."[15] Even studies on authority seem to emphasize the importance of the followers, for authority is perceived more correctly as an interactional relationship. The group possesses a freedom to respond and can exercise its responsibility in various ways. The interaction between leaders and followers affects the growth of the group and its ability to be effective according to its goals.

How can leadership be fostered and developed? Is there an appropriate leadership style for the last years of the twentieth century? The development of successful leaders is

[14]See Stogdill, pp. 107-108, for some interesting studies in this area. It is noted that authoritarian followers exercise more leadership in their groups and are not more submissive to leadership than non-authoritarian ones.

[15]Hollander, p. 290.

a matter of motivation as well as skill. Those who would be leaders must overcome their fear of greatness to give assent to the responsibilities of leadership. According to Maccoby, an ethic of self-development at all levels is necessary for a new and viable model of leadership.[16] In addition to competence, the essential components are creative thinking as well as knowledge, values, direction and spirit. A high degree of trust is also necessary if a leader is to be concerned about the release of potential in others. Leaders must begin to initiate new and varied approaches in many diverse situations. Since leaders are often asked to think and to act in terms of long-range goals, self-sacrifice is a prerequisite. The ability to grow, change, be flexible, interact, make things happen, understand humanity, have a global perspective, constitute some of the necessary ingredients of leadership. Whether education can encourage and foster the development of these qualities is sometimes questioned. However, the constant articulation of needs and of attributes may not only clarify but may begin to insure the development of new leaders for the world. The creation of an environment and an atmosphere where dreams can be fostered and ideas explored is essential if leaders are "to make conscious what lies unconscious among followers."[17] Leadership potentially has an elevating power when it identifies ideas and visions that can unite people. The development of such leaders is a difficult but urgent task.

If leadership qualities can be identified, then perhaps appropriate leadership styles can emerge. The leadership style of an individual can be described as "...the behavior pattern that a person exhibits when attempting to influence the activities of others."[18] Leadership style is a perception of others as much as an identifiable pattern of behavior in the leader. It is a complex phenomenon and a complex tool. For effective leadership today, Hersey and Blanchard suggest

[16]See Maccoby, p. 54.
[17]Burns, p. 40.
[18]Hersey and Blanchard, p. 233.

that leaders develop a broad range of styles in order to meet appropriately the demands of varied situations and groups.[19] These authors suggest that "telling" may be as appropriate as "delegating" depending on the situation and the level of maturity in the group.[20] Therefore flexibility in. approach is advocated as a consistent value. The contemporary focus on leadership indicates a shift in emphasis from power, position and authority to a relative situational quality and a participative involvement on the part of all. With this perspective in mind, we next examine the uniqueness of Christian leadership.

## Christian Leadership — The Essentials

Christian leadership is a specification of religious leadership,[21] and it has its roots within the biblical tradition. An understanding of the scriptural perspective is necessary in order effectively and uncompromisingly to integrate the insights of the broader study of leadership. For the purposes of this study, the Hebrew prophets and the early church are examined to identify the basic constituents of a religious or spiritual leadership. Then the essential components of such leadership for our time are suggested.

The Hebrew Bible is replete with examples of religious leadership, but to demonstrate some of the more consistent elements, the prophetic leaders Isaiah and Jeremiah are selected.[22] These two prophets are persons called by Yahweh and aware that call implies response and mission. However, while these convictions underlie the prophet's

[19] Hersey and Blanchard, pp. 233-234 and 257.

[20] See Hersey and Blanchard, p. 154, Table 7-1: "Leadership styles appropriate for various maturity levels." Compare this approach with Hall and Thompson's "Seven Levels of Leadership" p. 64. The entire chapter on "Developing Leadership: Consciousness and Value Theory Revisited" pp. 63-81 is valuable.

[21] The writer surveyed the literature of 10 years and was impressed with the quality and the quantity of writing in this area.

[22] For a full development of these points and complete scriptural documentation see the writer's article, "Isaiah and Jeremiah: Contrasts in Prophetic Leadership."

approach, there is a striking diversity in Isaiah's and Jeremiah's exercise of leadership. For example, while the individual prophet is conditioned by and responsive to the times, Isaiah prophesies during a period of impending threat, and Jeremiah witnesses the death of the nation.[23] For both, the religious significance of the political situation is continually assessed. The prophetic leader understands the spiritual and theological crisis within the threatening events and proclaims his message accordingly.

Furthermore, the prophet's religious convictions emanate in part from his understanding of the covenant. For Isaiah, it is the covenant of divine commitment in the Judean tradition originating in Abraham and David. For Jeremiah, it is the covenant of human obligation in the Ephraimite tradition originating in Moses. The theological understanding of the covenant and secondarily, the personality of the prophet, affects the leadership style so evident in the writings. For example, Isaiah emphasizes a hopeful message while Jeremiah preaches doom and destruction; these are theologically determined and personally witnessed. These prophetic leaders seem to be motivated by strong religious convictions; they are convinced that it is the word of Yahweh that they utter. Their theological convictions, while residing in a traditional understanding of the covenant, are reinterpreted for a new time and a new situation. The prophets are motivated and impelled by their religious convictions, and these seem to determine their involvement in and approach to the world of their day. Frequently, the prophet is perceived as a lonely figure who suffers, is rejected and yet endures in his ministry.[24] Both Isaiah and Jeremiah engage in a long ministry in Yahweh's service because of their faith, vision and hope.

---

[23]See R. E. Clements, *Isaiah 1-39*; John Bright, *Jeremiah*, for fine background and commentaries on these two books; also John Bright, *A History of Israel*.

[24]See Heschel, pp. 100 and 188. In addition to Heschel's two volumes *The Prophets*, von Rad's *The Message of the Prophets*, and Scott's *The Relevance of the Prophets*, Lindblom, *Prophecy in Ancient Israel*. These studies are particularly helpful for an understanding of the prophetic tradition.

These brief considerations offer some insight into the issue of religious leadership. If Isaiah and Jeremiah are valid examples of religious leadership, then such leadership must be grounded in a personal divine call that results in deep religious convictions. Theological understandings must be rooted in tradition but must also be capable of reinterpretation and development. Concrete situations must certainly be addressed, but from the insightful perspective of faith. Likewise, rejection and acceptance of the leader and the message should be evaluated in terms of the ultimate goal, not in terms of immediate response. The prophets of Israel, particularly Isaiah and Jeremiah, speak to spiritual leaders of every age: their diversity is refreshing; their style is realistic and encouraging; their courage and effectiveness is continually clarified with time.

The New Testament offers some further perspectives on religious leadership. Although the analysis of Paul's leadership is examined in detail in this study, a few select comments are offered in a preliminary way. While it is true that the focus and foundation of Christian leadership is Christ and that qualities such as forgiveness and compassion find their source in the gospels, the reality must be pursued more fully. For example, Jesus and the apostolic church portray the unique Christian exercise of authority as *diakonia* or service. New forms of relationship result from the conviction that Christ and the church are united in the Spirit. Furthermore, the death of Jesus becomes a starting point for the Christian paradox of power through weakness, life through death. These particular awarenesses enable Paul and the community to always give thanks to God in all situations (1Th 2:13; 5:18) and to constantly live in hope (1 Th 4:15-17). They also result in the challenge to imitate the pattern of the weakness and power of Christ so explicit in Paul's letters. Mutual responsibility within the community is also derived from these beliefs.

Leadership in the early church is directed toward the community and often exercised within the community. The community members are asked to discern and to test the authenticity of its manifestations. An underlying conviction is one that understands true leadership to be the work of the Spirit and not merely the reflection of human ability or talent. In fact, authority, so intimately connected with the exercise of leadership, is seen primarily as a gift of the Spirit. All such gifts are subject to the prime gift of the Spirit, which is love. The New Testament concept of power is also unique. Power is expressed in terms of love and of presence. The power of the gospel is the radical and transforming presence of the Lord. Secular positions are transormed (1 Th 5:12-13) when the essense of the Christian teaching is understood.

This study of Paul identifies a religious leadership that explicitly results from his call to preach the gospel. It will reveal a personal style of leadership and a situational approach to the various communities and individuals. It will also demonstrate the complexity of Paul as an early church leader and the versatile expression of his convictions in crisis and in peace.

From these biblical foundations and from an understanding of the church, some characteristics of Christian leadership can be suggested. John Wright points out that "...every kind of leadership in the Christian community is a sharing in the leadership of Christ by receiving from him the gift of the Holy Spirit."[25] The first essential component of Christian leadership is then, an understanding of the mystery of Christ and an authentic reinterpretation of his message for today. A second component is a radical openness to the working of the Spirit and an appreciation of the gifts of the Spirit within the community of faith. A number of implications are suggested in this understanding of Christian leadership. Christian leaders must operate on the level of gospel values, and these religious convictions must correct or complement appropriate leadership theory. Christian leaders and the community must likewise examine their own Christian awareness and all persons must challenge one another to the increasingly difficult task of preserving the quality of life so essential to the gospel. Spiritual leadership becomes the

[25]Wright, p. 12.

mutual response and responsibility of the community. In reality, this leadership, properly exercised, awakens others to their own call and commitment. It is an animating force and a mutual challenge. Christian leadership will, at times, be assertive and confronting because ultimate values are at stake. It will be a personal expression of charisms in and for the community. The result is the building up of the community which is the essence and heart of church. Prophetic insight, attentive listening, poverty for service and mutual trust permeate the group when spiritual leadership is exercised. These qualities foster the sensitive and supporting style of leadership so essential in a pluralistic church. An appreciation of weakness and strength, persuasion and conviction, integrity and flexibility is to be developed. Ecclesiology, which determines leadership style and an appropriate model or models of church, is vital. The ability to assess needs and sophisticated relational skills is also important. The religious leader must steadfastly create a confidence in the future for a church and a people who are experiencing crises. Christian leaders must also develop insight and resiliency so that mature human development is fostered in themselves and in others.[26] In many ways, the exercise of Christian leadership demands above average gifts and skills coupled with an extraordinary faith in the power of the Lord. The issue is raised regarding church leadership: does it incorporate the essentials of religious leadership?

It would appear that religious leadership is an authentic response to persons and to situations because of a personal, integrated, religious commitment. Padovano expresses it well:

> If a leader understands the nature of the church and the nature of people, the character of Christ and the character of the New Testament, if a leader is sensitive to love

---

[26]Essential to these points is the development of an appreciation of leisure which affects all dimensions of Christian life. See L. Doohan, "The Spiritual Value of Leisure."

and unafraid of faith, trusting about the future and confident with the present, such a leader will need to know no techniques in order to succeed. Every leader who cares about people is taught by them how to become the leader they need.[27]

## Approaches to the Study

The earliest New Testament documents are the Letters of Paul. These letters are written as early as 50 AD by the apostle and continue in the Pauline tradition until approximately 100 AD.[28] Since these manuscripts are letters, they contain copious amounts of information about people, situations, abuses, challenges, and issues of interest to particular communities. The communities addressed, such as Thessalonica, Corinth, Philippi, were well known in the ancient world and insight into their life-style and values is readily available in the results of current research.

Of special interest are the people portrayed in the letters, primarily Paul, but also Timothy, Titus, Silvanus and a host of others who are merely mentioned. Relationships between Paul and specific persons and communities can be discovered in the writings. In fact, the dynamic of leadership seems to be at work in the letters and a potential development or diversity of leadership styles is evident in Paul. A study of *Paul and Leadership* seems to be an appropriate undertaking since the sources of faith, such as scripture, and contemporary issues such as Christian leadership, must be approached from this dual perspective.

[27]Padovano, p. 224.

[28]The writer supports the dates resulting from the consensus of modern biblical scholarship; see Fitzmyer's review of Robinson's *Redating the New Testament*, in *Interpretation*, XXXIII, No. 3. The chart on p. 310 is very helpful for a comprehensive view of the question of date and authorship. Fine discussions are also available on particular letters, such as J. A. Bailey, "Who wrote II Thessalonians?" Generally the present writer followers Kummel's dating: I Thess 50, Gal 54-55, I Cor 54-55, II Cor 55-56, Rom 55-56, Phil 56-58. Romans may be later (57-58 - thus Robinson, Wikenhauser, Schmid, Fitzmyer), and the later date for Philippians is chosen over 53-55, which is consistent with current scholarship.

This study examines only those letters which unquestionably come from the apostle Paul, that is, 1 Thessalonians, Galatians, 1 and 2 Corinthians, Romans and Philippians.[29] The focus is on the person Paul in the correspondence, and the Paul of the *Acts of Apostles* is not a prime source. Theological and sociological issues are dealt with only in so far as they relate to an understanding of leadership. The perspective on controversies and issues raised in the letters is primarily that of Paul himself. Answers to current questions on church order and authority are very limited in the New Testament and are outside the scope of this study.

## The Religious Milieu of New Testament Times

In the analysis of Paul's letters, an understanding of the religious influences on his thought is essential. This next section will briefly assess the Jewish, Hellenistic and Roman influences and their significance.

The Jewish community during the time of Jesus and Paul was in a state of ferment. Paul being a Pharisaic Jew (Phil 3:4-5; Gal 1:13-14; 2:14-21) and living in diaspora is affected by Jewish as well as Hellenistic thought and perspectives.[30] However, according to Hengel, an assessment of the differences between Palestinian and Hellenistic Judaism is increasingly difficult. Within Jerusalem itself can be found an interest in the Hellenistic civilization if only among the aristocracy.[31] However, Judaic influences on Paul are seen in his approach to and understanding of sin, flesh, law, hope, obedience and resurrection. Likewise, Paul reflects the Jewish dissatisfaction with the priestly hierarchy in

---

[29]Philemon is eliminated because of its brevity and consequent limited value particularly to this study.

[30]See Davies, *Paul and Rabbinic Judaism,* for currents in Judaism affecting Paul. The work is impressive on this topic. Bornkamm, p. 10, distinguishes between the approaches in Jerusalem and in diaspora in regard to Jewish mission to the Gentiles.

[31]See Hengel, pp. 56 and 105.

Jerusalem by emphasizing communal relationships rather than ritual. From the Hellenistic Jewish environment is Paul's appreciation of persons as free, but finite human beings, as well as the value of interpersonal contentment. Paul builds on these insights as he proclaims the gospel.

It should also be understood that during Paul's time to be a Jew was both a religious and a political decision, a reality which had implications for his Gentile converts. Likewise, Judaism itself encompassed past, present and future in its understanding of itself, a perspective seen in Paul in regard to his theology and his approach to Christian life. Furthermore, the specific influence of Qumran on the New Testament has been established, and Paul possibly reflects this approach in his letters to the Corinthians.

Greek life and culture permeates the writings to a lesser degree perhaps, but the Stoic ideal (Phil 4:12) and Greek images are easily identified. Hengel notes that Hellenism is a complex phenomenon and embraces all aspects of life during this period.[32] There is a strong cross-cultural interest between Jews and Greeks, a perspective that must enter into the interpretation of Paul.

While Rome was the political power of the day and Roman citizenship was a valuble asset, some religious concepts are also significant. Among the Romans the tendency to ruler worship was a carry over from Hellenism. However, there are also the subtle influences in the letters as Paul contends with imprisonment and legal issues.

It is also important to remember that the New Testament is written during a period of questioning, turmoil and conflict. For Paul, the Judaizing tendencies of certain Jewish Christians and the ideas of pagan philosophers are at least challenges if not obstacles. The relationship between Jerusalem and the Gentile churches is developing slowly, and issues are being raised. The role of women is a source of tension and is affected by religious and cultural perspec-

---

[32]See Hengel, p.3.

tives. Even the spoken and written languages of the day reflect the broad and changing influences of the Jewish, Greek and Roman world. The same is true of the development of leadership styles in the early church. Paul's task, as a Jew influenced by the world around him, is to understand and to utilize his background and experience to live and to proclaim the Christian gospel in a very diversified but alive environment.

## A Perspective on Paul

As a result of the examination of the crises in the church, and the contemporary views on leadership and religious leadership, there is need for future directions and for a further clarification of principles. Furthermore, in the brief analysis of the situation and influences in the early church, the terminology and religious background of the period, the apostle Paul is identified as a product and a reflection of his times. However, if the contemporary situation and the early Christian situation share parallels or similarities, and if Paul sufficiently challenges the primitive churches, his leadership approach may offer prophetic insight into a new situation as well as his own. This dual perspective of the early Christian community and the contemporary church is the focus of this research, and the study has potential value in both these areas.

Paul's letters, written during his missionary journeys deal not only with growth issues, but often address crises within the early Christian communities. The church and groups in crisis situations today may learn from his mistakes and his leadership.

Paul's letters reveal changes and development in theology, and flexibility in leadership style. The gospel is adapted to a Gentile audience and culture. Paul's writing spans almost a decade and comparisons and contrasts can be made. The relationships with co-workers and the roles among the leaders and members of the community reveal a rich diversity. Mutual responsibility seems to be a major factor in church development. This dynamism and growth in the early church offer significant perspectives for a church today that is attempting creatively to deal with changing roles and ministries. Ministry in the New Testament addresses new needs, and the theme of service permeates the writings of Paul.

In passing on the tradition, Paul demonstrates a reverence for and a creative utilization of what has been received. It would appear that the process as well as the proclamation is relevant for today.

Paul's personality is evident in his letters, especially 2 Corinthians, Galatians, Philippians, and a personal relationship with the communities is a continual priority. When he undergoes a religious conversion from Judaism to being a follower of the Lord, his religious convictions redirect his life and ministry in the early church.

Certainly Paul can offer some insights into the understanding of Christian leadership today, as the motivations, approaches and effectiveness of this formidable figure in the early church are uncovered through study of his own letters. Paul, if in touch with his times and creatively ahead of his times, can also speak prophetically to this era.

# 1

# EARLY LEADERSHIP IN PAUL: THE FIRST LETTER TO THE THESSALONIANS

"Paul, Silvanus, Timothy, to the church of the Thessalonians in God the Father and the Lord Jesus Christ" (1 Th1:1). With these simple, direct words, the dawn of a new era in gospel proclamation began. Paul, in making a decision to write makes this means of communication an extension of his apostolic authority as an apostle of Jesus Christ and undertakes to create a community by means of an apostolic letter. In addressing the church, that is the assembly of Christians, and not individuals, Paul initiates a pattern that will be his normal practice. In this earliest New Testament writing, not only is there a glimpse of a young and fervent community some twenty years after the resurrection of Jesus, but a visual image of Paul is recorded in this stage of his work in the church. The letter to the Thessalonians has a charm and an appeal in the very joy and approval that run through it. Even the admonitions are given in a surprisingly gentle way, so that any existing shortcomings of the church seem very small (1:9-10).[1] In the study of the letter to the Thessalonians, a perspective on letters and letter writing is presented. Following these intro-

---

[1] Munck, "1 Thess. 1:9-10...," p. 97.

ductory comments, the situation is described, issues are identified and the interaction assessed. It is Paul, the emerging leader that is encountered. In the writing itself he is, and will continue to be, "...an instinctive master of this form of the art of personal communication.[2]"

Paul is indeed desirous of personal communication and personal contact with the Thessalonian community, and can say to them: "(I)...endeavored more eagerly and with great desire to see you face to face; because we wanted to come to you — I, Paul, again and again..." (2:17-18). In fact, he uses the term "bereft of you" which indicates severe deprivation and desolation, "being made orphans" and "having been torn away from you." Because of this continued difficult state that he experiences, he has the great desire to return to the community. Indeed, Paul separates himself from his own race and finds a new family in his converts. He longs and cares for them in a deep and personal way.[3] This personal concern eventually leads Paul to utilize letter writing as a substitute for a visit.

Because of the importance he attaches to the letter and the leadership he exerts through the written word, Paul can say I "adjure you by the Lord that this letter be read to all the brethren" (5:27). In the use of such strong language, Paul not only insured that the letter reaches everyone in the community but intended to accomplish what a visit should. Furthermore, the letter has a formal character about it, being an apostolic communication. Paul believes that the Lord is revealing himself through him to the Thessalonians. Paul's perception of himself as a religious leader and the importance of his mission is glimpsed in this unique command. In fact:

> ...the public reading of the letter, one day to be acknowledged as pertaining to the Scriptures of the new people of God, was an event which we can qualify as liturgical. The very reading of 1 Thess. allowed the believers of Thessa-

[2]Perrin, *The New Testament*, p. 97.
[3]Best, *Thess* p. 125.

lonica to come into existence as the Church of God (1 Thess 2:14).[4]

The letter is creative of community and Paul understands this dimension early in his career. In 1 Thess 5:27 is the only explicit statement directing the reading of any of the Pauline letters in a liturgical context. This fact indicates the growth in Paul's stature as his writing and missionary work continue. There is no need to "adjure" the community or its leaders in this regard in the later correspondence.

The letters of Paul are usually characterized as having originality and diversity, an occasional or situational origin with universal implications. They are the official acts of an apostle. In addition, they are the letters of an experienced missionary who is accustomed to preaching and to instructing. This background of experience is also true of 1 Thessalonians although Paul may only recently have become aware of his explicit mission to the Gentiles.[5] Furthermore, within this brief letter to the Thessalonians, one finds a closer connection with the origin of the church than in almost any other New Testament writing. For this reason, 1 Thessalonians offers some unique insights into the earliest issues in the church and the beginnings of Christian theological reflection. One of these major issues which draws Paul's attention and concern is eschatology. While much of Paul's reflection on the end times can be attributed to his Pharisaic background and the influence of the Hellenistic environment, there is a uniqueness in Paul's understanding of this topic. One author comments: "The most fundamentally new thing in Paul's eschatology is his insight that the sending, death upon the cross, and resurrection of Jesus constitute the turning point in the ages."[6] The first letter to the Thessalonians already reflects this awareness (4:14; 5:9) even

---

[4]Collins, p. 62.

[5]See Perrin, *The New Testament*, pp. 94f., for an insightful hypothesis on Paul's awareness of Gentile mission. Perrin accounts for the seemingly unsuccessful years between Paul's conversion and his first letter by his missionary activity being directed primarily to Jews. Only with his contacts in Antioch and after the Jerusalem Council does Paul consciously move to the Gentiles.

[6]Bornkamm, *Paul*, p. 199.

though a full development will emerge only in the later correspondence.

Paul in writing his letters, utilizes the accepted form of his day. In his very use of the typically Hellenistic form, he conveys his sense of the importance of his correspondence. However, in 1 Thessalonians the existing letter form is adapted from a Christian perspective. Paul utilizes what is available to him, but leaves his own creative imprint. For example, the thanksgiving which is long in this letter (1:2 -3:13) is not a regular feature in contemporary letters. However, it is an intrinsic part of 1 Thessalonians. In addition, the greeting itself is neither Jewish nor Greek but distinctively Christian. Paul, not only writes but creatively writes, and in his early correspondence he demonstrates and reveals the leadership potential which will change and develop as he continues his mission in the church. Within the letter to the Thessalonians the situation, issues and interaction are examined with a view to the assessment of the early leadership of Paul.

## The Situation

The Thessalonian situation is presented with a particular focus on the interrelationship of the co-workers, the composition of the community and the presence of opposition. It is from Corinth, in 50 AD during the second missionary journey, that Paul writes to his community at Thessalonica. The situation and the concerns of this community are vital to an understanding of Paul as a leader, for in addition to the literary and teaching methods of his day, the environment itself provides a means by which Paul expresses his thought. Indeed, the sociological context affects Paul's theological ideas, and situation often defines his leadership response.

Paul apparently departed suddenly from Thessalonica, a leave which could possibly be interpreted as desertion of the community. However, Paul's stay in Thessalonica was long enough to receive financial help from Philippi (2:9) and to refer to his own example (1:6; 2:9). The community knew him and would not easily misinterpret his actions. The

Thessalonians are basically on the right path in their Christian life and need only some stimulation and direction a short time after their conversion (1:2). Paul is aware that the fruits of his visit and of his work still endure (2:1) and so the situation elicits a positive tone from the founder of the community. This situation is unique in Paul's experience, with only the Philippian letter on a par. Paul has a relatively easy leadership role in a problem-free Christian community.

In the opening verse of the letter, Paul indicates that he writes in the name of all three apostles, and Silvanus and Timothy are introduced as some of Paul's colleagues and co-workers. Silvanus, the Silas of Acts, is one of the leading persons in the Jerusalem church who in Acts is sent to Antioch (Acts 15:22f). He is Paul's companion on the second journey as Barnabas was on the first journey, and in this capacity is co-founder of the churches in Macedonia. Paul and Silvanus initially travel to Philippi and then on to Thessalonica (Acts 17:1-10). Timothy, the son of a Jewish mother and a Greek father (Acts 16:1-3) joins Paul in Lystra during the second journey, and becomes an important collaborator. He can best be described as an assistant, or a junior companion, and Paul will frequently send him on missions (3:2; 1 Co 4:17; Phil 2:19, 23). The young Timothy is called a brother by Paul (3:2), and is a likely choice to send to Thessalonica because the people there know him. Paul seems to respect his co-workers and even writes 1 Thessalonians on the basis of what he hears from Timothy (3:6), as well as from his own knowledge of Thessalonica and the usual development of young Christian communities. Paul's use of Timothy in such a respected manner and his commissioning of Timothy to establish and to exhort the community in faith (3:2), indicates Paul's confidence in sharing his mission with his co-workers, even those who are lower in rank or status. This quality is essential in leadership, although Paul will always remain the directing force in the missionary work to the churches. Because of his own attitude, Paul exhorts this community to demonstrate some of these same qualities toward those who "labor among you, give aid to you" and "admonish you" (5:12).

Paul also reminds the community of how he and his co-workers gave instruction (4:2) and how they labored and toiled among them (2:9). It can easily be overlooked that "Paul was essentially a part-time, not a full-time missionary, carrying on his evangelistic and pastoral activities alongside the practice of his trade. This makes his achievements all the more extraordinary!"[7] Paul's co-workers are thus vital to his mission since his time is limited or divided. The leader, Paul, uses these persons well and is able to delegate responsibility when it is indicated (3:2).

The missionaries came to Thessalonica after being shamefully treated at Philippi, and once they arrived in Thessalonica, they preached in the face of great opposition (2:2; see Acts 16:22-24). Thessalonica is a strategically located port city in Macedonia with a small Jewish population and a large number of Gentile converts to Christianity (Acts 17:1-9). Indeed, the community received the word in affection and in joy (1:6), becoming such an example in the regions of Macedonia and Achaia that Paul can say, that their faith has gone forth everywhere (1:8). They "turned to God from idols" (1:9), and subsequently suffered for their faith (2:14-15). It is to this community that Paul writes not too long after his visit although his success with them is far from being assured. Indeed, leadership itself "has a relative quality about it: it is relative to the time, the situation, the needs."[8] Paul must be aware of the Gentile audience who may find it difficult to obey the word of the apostles without discussion or argument. Likewise, conversion itself costs the community. Because civic and social life are closely bound up with paganism, the break is sharp and costly. Paul gives a rather extensive description of evangelizing this Gentile community and seems to be keenly aware of their needs (2:1-12). He speaks of his sincerity (2:1-4), integrity (2:5-8), apostolic unselfishness (2:9-10), and fatherly concern (2:11-

---

[7]Banks, p. 153; also see Hock, pp. 444-450, for the importance of the workshop in missionary activity. The workshop is seen as the social setting of a portion of Paul's missionary work.

[8]Putrow, p. 103.

12), and thereby portrays himself in terms that will appeal to the community. He also defends himself against any charges against his integrity, or suggestive of monetary gain. Paul also describes Jesus as savior from heaven rather than in Jewish Messianic terms. It is true for Paul at this early stage that "the qualities, characteristics, and skills required in a leader are determined to a large extent by the demands of the situation in which he is to function as a leader."[9]

It is in the midst of opposition as well as in a non-Jewish community that Paul preaches and his ministry does not seem to be in vain (2:1). What kind of opposition does Paul meet in Thessalonica? What is its origin? Are there identifiable opposing groups at this early stage in his ministry? A number of possible opposition groups are discussed by the exegetes such as the judaizers, spiritual enthusiasts, gnostics and Jews. In 1:14, Paul acknowledges that the community "suffered the same things from your own countrymen as they (the churches in Judea) did from the Jews.". A conclusion is drawn: "the letter allows us to conclude that the church was composed of Gentile Christians (1 Thess 1:9f) and that its persecutors were Gentiles."[10]

Opposition and afflictions are perceived to be part of Christian existence. As Paul said: "This is to be our lot. For when we were with you, we told you beforehand that we were to suffer affliction; just as it has come to pass" (3:3-4). While the community is experiencing affliction and opposition, the letter does not appear to indicate any Christian agitators opposing the apostle. Paul has to contend with "the miracle-workers of paganism" and defends the legitimacy of his apostleship with this group.

However, the Jews seem to be the object of a surprising attack (2:15-16). "To say that the Jews were enemies of their fellow men echoes the common misunderstanding and suspicion of them in the ancient world, and is unexpected on

[9]Stogdill, p. 62.

[10]Bornkamm, *Paul*, p. 63; see Moore, p. 44, where he describes the troublemakers as "kith and kin."

[11]Grayston, p. 72.

the lips of a devout Jew."[11] There is a growing separation between Jews and Jewish followers of Jesus even at this early date. Paul does seem to be the object of a slanderous campaign in his absence with unworthy motives and dishonorable purposes attributed to him. However, it has been pointed out that Paul's outburst against the Jews is in sharp contrast to his positive desire for them in Romans 9-11. While Paul suffers at their hands, his understandable attack seems to be exaggerated. Not only is the statement exaggerated, but also it is not a persistent, passionate or retaliatory statement. One author comments: "The enemy, if there really is one, is vague, and the defense can be nothing other than vague; there is no passion as there is in so many of Paul's other letters because there is no group against which Paul can be passionate."[12]

Perhaps, Paul in 1 Thessalonians can better be described as "a good pastor counselling the congregation, and discussing theological problems (e.g. the end) only as they emerge from pastoral situations."[13] Since he is not arguing with a defined and formidable opposition, his tone and his approach are mild and calm. Paul the leader knows and understands the community situation and responds to it in 1 Thessalonians.

## The Issues

In the letter to the Thessalonians, there is no presentation of an abstract doctrine, no visible opposition to quell, and no serious abuse. Rather, it is the initial preaching to the community which must be reinforced by further clarifications and admonitions. Paul understands the situation and responds accordingly. He offers sound advice of a pastoral nature that indicates the focus and direction of his own missionary work. While there is no systematic instruction in this writing, a personal and original witness to Pauline

[12]Best, p.22.
[13]Best, p. 23.

missionary work is evident in the letter. Paul may indeed be anticipating some problems or sense some anti-social attitudes that are potentially problematic. These matters or concerns are synthesized in several ways, but can be viewed under the following categories: 1) the parousia and the concern in the community regarding their dead (4:13f); 2) life in the community with an emphasis on moral integrity, mutual love and mutual responsibility (4:4f; 4:9f); 3) minor matters concerning the relationship of the community to others. Again, the situational impact is evident in the issues, teachings and exhortations. In a spectrum of mundane matters and intermittent squabbles, Paul's letters bear the unmistakable imprint of their world. Thessalonians is certainly no exception to this general assessment.

Paul and the community are concerned with the parousia and the final resurrection, a concern which is heightened because some in the community have already died. It may seem strange that the fact of the death of some Christians is an issue, but many of "...the earliest Christians maintained that they were already risen, and therefore did not at first expect death for themselves, or accept it as normal" (4:13f).[14]

Paul presents his eschatological teaching as "the word of the Lord" and uses the prevailing imagery of his day to express his thought. The teaching is very positive and hopeful not only regarding the dead but also regarding the fate of the entire community. "The dead in Christ will rise first; then we who are alive, who are left, shall be caught up together with them in the clouds to meet the Lord in the air; and so we shall always be with the Lord" (4:16-17).

The second coming seems to be in the near future. However, Paul gives a fully developed response and removes all speculations and unfounded fears about their future before God (5:1-11). As an early Christian leader, Paul responds not only to the specific issue he is questioned about, but to the underlying fears of his converts. Paul soon changes his views on the nearness of the parousia but he always recog-

[14]Mearns, p. 141.

nizes the issues at stake. In 1 Thessalonians, a theological misunderstanding raises some concrete questions in the community and Paul must respond. The questions regarding the end may also give a further indication about the composition of the community itself, if as has been suggested, "the eschatological expectation of the end was above all a matter for the lower classes who bore the whole burden of an insecure social existence."[15] The Thessalonians may consist largely of this group.

Life in the community is another identifiable issue with the exhortations focusing on immorality (4:3b-6), mutual responsibility (4:11-12; 5:11) and respect toward leaders (5:12-13). Paul probably raises all these issues because of his awareness of the Gentile world and of human weakness. Immorality and sexual promiscuity were common in the pagan society of Paul's day, and he is aware of the lower standards and the moral dangers for the community. In a somewhat sweeping statement about the Gentiles, there is a reasonable assessment of the dangers would be recognized by the recipients of the letter. Furthermore, Paul reminds the community of his own teaching while in their midst and again challenges them to live quietly, to mind their own affairs and to continue manual work (4:11).

Although the Greeks generally looked on certain types of work as demeaning, Paul does not see it in this way, and so he challenges the idle (5:14). He uses himself as an example to foster responsible action in this area (2:9). It is interesting to note that the term "idle" also pertains "to those who create disorder."[16] Paul seems to address a broad spectrum of potential deterrents to the peace and harmony of the community. He also places responsibility for the preservation of a quality Christian life with the members themselves, since they are to continue to encourage and to build up one another (5:11). Paul already begins to differentiate and to clarify his role in relation to the followers, for comforting and strengthening one another is their task (4:18).

[15]Hengel, *Judaism and Hellenism*, p. 254.

[16]Roetzel, p. 144, footnote 2; see 1 Cor 14:40.

Finally, in a very pastoral section of the letter (5:12-22), Paul begins with three exhortations that reflect certain activities or functions within the community. Regarding the leaders within the group, who labor and admonish the community (5:12), they are challenged "to respect" and "to esteem them very highly in love because of their work" (5:12-13). Exegetes concur that at this early time in the church's life, functions and activities are differentiated but that the idea of an official would be foreign. It is noteworthy that Paul exhorts the followers to respect and esteem their leaders "because of their work" (5:13), or in other words, because of the way they function within the community. Leaders must earn respect and do not automatically have it because of position; followers must offer respect to leaders because of the way they exercise their leadership in the group. Paul insightfully raises the issue of a right and fruitful relationship between leaders and followers even though the tone of the letter does not indicate a serious rift within the community between leaders and people. These exhortations should be seen within the context of the diversity of spiritual gifts given to all members of the community (2:19f). Other letters such as 1 Corinthians and Romans develop the idea of charism, and continue to demonstrate the expectation of Paul that all Christians possess spiritual gifts (see 1 Cor 7:7; 12:1,4,11; 14:1; Rm 12:6).

Among the other issues in Thessalonians are Paul's attitude toward the Jews (2:15-16) and the destiny of the Gentiles. These two issues affect almost every missionary endeavor of the apostle to the Gentiles. In addition, in Thessalonica the "...attitude to the pagans and Jews in their own city, from whom they had endured persecution, and with whom they were rubbing shoulders every day" was a problem for the community as well (3:12).[17] These might be considered minor matters in one sense because Paul does not spend much time in this letter dealing with the issue of the relationship between Jew and Gentile. However, it will

[17]Whiteley, p. 56.

be an ongoing issue for Paul and all the Christian communities on a theological and existential level. Paul's early awareness is therefore significant.

## Interaction and Response

As has been demonstrated, Paul utilizes letter writing as an essential component of his missionary activity and in the letters, a discovery of the unique situation of the community and various indications of the issues are evident. Although 1 Thessalonians is rather brief, the text does facilitate a glimpse of the early interactions between a religious leader and his community. The responsiveness of Paul is explored in terms of his use of exhortations, his claims of authority, his perspective on community, his dealing with the question of the parousia and on the beginning signs of alienation.

Paul builds on his earlier experience of preaching and of teaching within the Thessalonian community. "In ever new phrases the apostle reminds them of these facts: 'you know' (1:5; 2:1ff) 'you remember' (2:9), 'you are witnesses' (2:10). These all seem to be entirely fresh recollections."[18] With his previous personal presence to the community in mind and with what he knows of the community from Timothy, Paul spends the bulk of chapters four and five exhorting the community. The exhortations, as the entire letter, reflect his pastoral concern. Paul in a very real sense forsees the unforseeable and knows the unknowable when he challenges the community along the lines of potential problem areas. One author concludes: "It is moreover wholly in the style of Paul to set down a list of injunctions without having a precise group in mind each time, but rather an attitude which any Christian might have ..."[19]

[18]Kummel, p. 184.
[19]Best, p. 231.

These universal, though not vague challenges speak of a leader who anticipates the future difficulties of the Christian community. He also anticipates the corrective and already instills in the Thessalonians a keen sense of their own responsibility to one another and to community growth: "You...admonish the idle, encourage the fainthearted, help the weak, be patient with them all" (5:14).

"The terms he employs are most frequently words of exhortation and appeal, rather than command or decree,"[20] but the point is made. How do the followers respond to the general exhortations given by Paul? How will they continue to assume their own responsibility to "encourage," "build one another up" and "test everything" or discern? (5:11,20) Perhaps Paul's personal attitude toward the community will offer an indication.

The community at Thessalonica, as the one in Philippi, is very much a source of joy for the apostle who is happy to see their faith grow and develop. Paul speaks personally, to "each one of you." Indeed, "Paul had enough respect for each person to refrain from treating all alike."[21] He affirms the community (1:8) and affirmation is certainly a way of ensuring not only followership but also growth. Furthermore, Paul seems to indicate a deep affection for the community in his choice of terms and images; e.g. brethren (1:4 and passim), gentle "as a nurse taking care of her children" (2:7), "affectionately desirous of you...you have become very dear to us"(2:8), "a father with his children" (2:11). These terms "reveal the heart of Paul - father, nurse, apostle, fellow-believer, one who builds up and encourages those under attack (cf. 1 Thess 2:17; 3:5-10; 4:1)."[22] However, it should be noted that Paul is not condescending in his attitude toward the community, because Paul's model is the

---

[20] Banks, pp. 176-177. The author goes on to say: "By far the most common term used by him in these contexts is *parakalein* "appeal', which is used some 23 times in his writings. This parallels the use of the term *peitho*, 'persuade' or 'convince', in contexts where his preaching to outsiders is in view."

[21] Whiteley, p.44.

[22] Reese, p. xv.

relationship of adult child with its parent. Paul also responds in an intensely personal way that speaks of his deep human and Christian convictions. Reese can say: "The message of these letters is communicated prayerfully as a fruit of Paul's own life in Christ and as an expression of his apostolic concern for those he invited to believe."[23]

Praying constantly (1:3; 2:13; 5:17), the attitude of Paul and the community can sensitize the community to God's action in Paul and in themselves, thereby ensuring a high degree of followership. It would appear, then, that "instead of the harsh polemic seen elsewhere, this letter blossoms with assurance and comfort, gentle admonition and conciliation, encouragement and pastoral care."[24] Permeating his relationship and his encouragement is an underlying religious conviction: "...this is the will of God, your sanctification" (4:3a). This conviction is closely related to Paul's understanding of his role as a religious leader.

Paul acts, teaches and responds because "our gospel came to you not only in word, but also in power and in the Holy Spirit with full conviction" (1:5a). He perceives himself as "approved by God to be entrusted with the gospel," and so he speaks..." (2:4). He exhorts "in the Lord Jesus" (4:1) and is convinced that the word he preaches is "the word of God" (2:13). In all of these statements, whether Paul is speaking of gospel or word,[25] he bases his authority and his entire ministry on what he has received from the Lord. There is a religious conviction, a lived religious conviction, in the apostle Paul. The Thessalonians likewise are to be aware that more than a human response and interaction is at work in Paul and also in them: "...the word of God,...is at work in you believers" (2:13). Said another way: "the gospel originates with God, is about Christ, and is presented by

---

[23]Reese, p. xv.

[24]Roetzel, p. 52.

[25]See Fitzmyer, "Gospel...," p. 341, where he notes that "gospel" and "word" are often used synonymously by Paul.

Paul and his associates."[26] For this reason, Paul consistently thanks God, who speaks through him, and not necessarily the Thessalonians who respond (2:13). It is from God that all emanates and Paul's authority is best perceived in this context (4:1). Having established the foundations of his religious leadership and having reminded the Thessalonians of the Christian context of their lives, Paul responds to the issues that were identified earlier.

The apostle reflects on the "coming of the Lord Jesus" in the context of the holiness of the believers (3:13). When speaking of the ultimate destiny of the community, he describes it not as wrath, but as "salvation through our Lord Jesus Christ" (5:9). The Christians at Thessalonica are waiting for "his Son from heaven" since their conversion (1:9), and this very expectation is identified as a part of the earliest kerygma, or proclamation. However, the community is anxious about those members who have died, and Paul addresses the issue because he would not have them ignorant or grieving as others who have no hope (4:13). The parousia teaching itself (4:15-17) is an echo of a quote from Jesus, and couched in Old Testament apocalyptic and Hellenistic imagery. However, while Paul uses the traditions, the thought patterns, language and imagery of his day, his leadership response is more clearly seen in the content of the instruction itself. Indeed,

> Paul's primary purpose in writing is not to enunciate doctrine but to reassure them in respect of this...(he) writes as a pastor rather than a theologian, but all good pastoral counselling is based on, and contains, theological teaching and is not mere consolation.[27]

There is a Christian confidence in Paul as he reassures the community. He reassures them regarding the dead, and points out that the dead will have no advantage over them.

[26]Best, p. 74.

[27]Best, pp. 180-181.

He then speaks of their own position in the parousia and describes all believers as being "with the Lord" (4:17). "This is encouragement indeed, and encouragement to be shared."[28] Paul seems to portray a dramatic second coming, present some prior teaching and then move on to new ideas which offer real hope. With this community he counters any despair and centers his new vision of the parousia on their own readiness and preparation for the event (5:1-11). It is interesting that Paul brushes aside insignificant or inappropriate questions: "But as to the times and the seasons, brethren, you have no need to have anything written to you" (5:1). For Paul does not write to satisfy curiosity concerning even perfectly legitimate questions, but to address the pastoral needs of the Christians at Thessalonica. He therefore emphasizes "the continued seriousness of the event, reassures the faithful that they are bound for salvation, and exhorts them to readiness" (5:1-11).[29] The leader Paul can identify the significant elements within an issue and make a priority the real or underlying questions that necessitate a response. He employs as his guideline what is essential and what is helpful for Christian existence. Allaying fears and offering hope seem essential, while the incidental date of the parousia is a matter of idle curiosity. In fact, Paul seems almost abrupt in dealing with what he considers a non-issue (5:1ff). This characteristic or potential flaw in Paul's response is examined in the ensuing correspondence. However, even if Paul is momentarily irritated, he quickly recalls what the community knows well (5:2), and then identifies the clear difference between the Christian and pagan. It is a difference of being and not of degree. He offers the supreme challenge to live differently, realizing that his very life will find its consummation in the parousia. "The mystery of completion thus encounters a Christian as a threat and as a promise. The day of the Lord as a threat calls for vigilance

---

[28]Montague, p. 22.

[29]Plevnik, p. 87; see Rigaux, *Thessaloniciens*, pp. 552-553, as noted in footnote 64 in the article.

and sobriety. The day of the Lord as salvation guides and inspires Christian hope."[30]
The hope offered here by the religious leader Paul is a realistic hope. He is clearly convinced that the best preparation for the day of the Lord is an authentic Christian existence. This authentic existence is lived out within the community; and so Paul reflects on his relationship to the converts, and responds to any potential flaw in community life.

Paul addresses the Thessalonians as brethren, a term of endearment and affection, fourteen times in this letter. So personal and good is his relationship with them that he uses himself as a model and example (1:6). The community is his boast and his crown (2:19-20), and Paul's joy and thanksgiving flows from a realization of God's activity in them (3:9). Paul equates life for himself with the community's fidelity to the Lord (3:8). Community members give him a new lease on life because of their lived faith. How close and deep is the relationship between Paul and the community (2:8) because of the faith they share (1:8). "Paul's life is bound up with the vigour of Christian life on the Churches."[31]

It is within the context of his own personal relationship with and his attitude toward the community that Paul's challenges to the Thessalonians can best be understood. The community remembers Paul affectionately (3:6), and he is aware of this response as he writes. Because of a good mutual relationship, Paul expects that he will be understood and not misinterpreted. Therefore, he gives general instruction on morality (4:3b-6), expecting a positive response to his attempts to forewarn the community. He affirms the community, but in the affirmation challenges them to deeper growth and development (4:9-10). Although he says that "concerning love of the brethren you have no need to have anyone write to you" (4:9), Paul follows this compliment with specific admonitions on appropriate responses in

---

[30] Plevnik, p. 90.
[31] Whiteley, p. 54.

the community. At first, Paul speaks to persons within the community on their own attitudes to life: "live quietly," "mind your own affairs," "work with your hands," "be dependent on no one"(4:11-12). Paul is warning against any disruptive attitudes that will influence and affect the peace and harmony of the community. The effectiveness of the Christian witness to outsiders is dependent on the quality of their basic personal and communal attitudes. Paul makes a public relations point to a community accused of having troublemakers in its midst. But whether he has their past history, present and future difficulties in mind, Paul always focuses on relationships with God and with each other as the essence of Christianity. Of the many ways God communicates himself to humankind, His revelation through persons is a prime orientation for Paul. Therefore, in responding to situations of normal human weakness, Paul is protecting the essence of the existential experience of Christianity. He would expect the challenges on community life to be heard because of his care in expressing them and because of the Thessalonians own deep commitment to the Lord.

Paul then urges the community to assume its responsibility "to encourage one another and to build one another up" (5:11). Mutual responsibility is advocated, and in this exhortation, Paul begins to reflect on the relationship between leaders and followers. He gives a teaching (5:1-10) and sees the community assuming its role in interpreting the message in the daily situations of Christian living. A principle is emerging, "with respect to each of the areas of community life...responsibility lies with every member to play his (her) part in the leadership of the community."[32] In fact, there are explicit challenges along the lines of leadership (5:11-12). Esteem and love should be given to leaders, and their value readily acknowledged because of the quality of their work. Again mutual responsibility is fostered and a leadership-followership dynamic is set in motion in the Christian community. Any security in a status-position is

[32]Banks, p. 141.

unacceptable among Christians and the authority of the
"significant persons...present in Paul's communities-
...comes from the ministry discharged by them in the community."[33] Leadership as gift and service is the focus.
Consequently, Paul intends an ongoing mutual challenge.
The context of the relationship between leader and followers is not only gift, but also love: "Only love can create a true
and fruitful relationship in the whole community between
those who exercise responsibility and those over whom they
exercise it."[34]

Further exhortations are given on community life (5:14-
22), but in the midst of these concrete responsibilities is the
specific mention of prayer and thanksgiving (5:17-18). This
reminder reinforces the essence of Christian community as a
qualitatively different experience. The Thessalonians,
because of their deep faith commitment, presumably have
the ability continually to focus on essentials. In his interaction with the community, Paul relies heavily on his own
personal relationship to them, and their respect for him.
From this starting point, he challenges the community to
grow and to strengthen its relationships with all persons and
more specifically with the leaders in their midst. Because of
a personal respect and a Christian commitment, Paul could
anticipate a positive response to his admonition.

Paul's dynamic of leadership is also seen in what he
defends himself against, namely: false leadership (2:3),
deceit (2:3), greed (2:5), seeking personal glory (2:6), allowing himself to be supported by the congregation (2:7) and
flattery and pleasing of persons (2:4f). Paul is desirous of
establishing and/ or maintaining his credibility to ensure a
good reception of his letter. On another level, Paul's defense
also highlights inappropriate attitudes in the community,
and subtly challenges the brethren. Furthermore, Paul's
defense is indicative of the alienation he experiences from
his own people. These accusations against Paul may origi-

[33]Banks, p. 151.
[34]Best, p. 227.

nate with the Jews. His new religious convictions open him to misunderstanding from Jews and Gentiles as he "moves between two worlds...(and experiences) two different language-areas and cultures."[35] While Paul does indeed defend himself, he does not offer a concrete attack on groups or individuals. A general response to vague opposition is the tenor of 1 Thessalonians. On a leadership level, Paul is responding to issues and to ideas and not to specific people. This approach usually elicits a positive response. Since there are seemingly no specific groups or persons under attack in the community, this kind of response is appropriate.

Although only the first letter to the Thessalonians is under examination, the scripture text reveals a dynamic at work between Paul and the community. The situation, the issues and the interactions have been identified, and now contribute to an understanding and assessment of Paul's early leadership.

## Assessment of Paul's Leadership

In 1 Thessalonians, Paul the leader is at work and an assessment of some of the components of his emerging leadership style is possible. As a religious leader, Paul presents a vision of Christian life and reflects on his authority to do so. He is interested in the relational component of community living, emphasizing attitudes and mutual responsibility. While many factors contribute to Paul's initial success as a leader, the important constituents of his early approach are identified.

In this first writing, Paul already presents a Christian *vision* of life to his fledgling community. The church at Thessalonica is constituted as such because it is "...in God the Father and the Lord Jesus Christ" (1:1). Consequently, it is God who is to be thanked for everything, including the

---

[35] Hengel, *Judaism and Hellenism*, p. 82.

Thessalonians' initial acceptance of the Christian gospel (2:13). The reality of God's continual activity is consistently presented by Paul and it is this activity of the Lord Himself that is responsible for the Christian growth of the community (3:12). The believers are different in essence and in being from their pagan neighbors; they are "...sons of light and sons of the day" (5:5). Paul's vision always revolves around this central core of Christian existence, namely, God's presence to and God's activity in the community of faith. Paul's understanding is continually clarified because he actually "...'thinks' before God as much as he acts before him; his whole life is continually held in the presence of God."[36] This openness to God is the essence of religious leadership and some implications certainly follow for Paul and for the community. If God is ultimately responsible for Christian life and growth (5:23-24), then Paul can rightly present the consequences of his vision in terms of always living in hope (4:15-17). Also, Christian people and a Christian community can rely on more than their own human potential because God is at work in them. This realization itself offers hope. Furthermore, Christians are able to give thanks in all circumstances (5:18), because their values and their perspective are different. A Christian vision of life transforms the ordinary experiences of life, creates new attitudes and challenges old values. This reality is frequently suggested by Paul. The qualitative difference is *agapé* or Christian love (5:12-13). Paul is convinced of the primacy of love in God and in persons.[37] When leadership and life are viewed from a Christian perspective, it is always love which makes them distinctively Christian.

Because of his vision, Paul challenges the community to aspire to greatness in their daily life (4:11). A good leadership principle underlies the great visionary challenges of

---

[36]Best, p. 70.

[37]See Spicq, *Agapé*, Vol. II, p. 93 (and passim). He asserts that Paul's insight into the essence of *agapé* or Christian love is as insightful in 1 Thess as in his later letters. There is no real progression in this concept, but the essence of *agape* was grasped early by Paul. It is centered in Calvary and is Paul's chief revelation.

Paul, for he understands well that small plans or small ideas have little power to move people. However, creative ideas and broad vision have the power to unite and to move people even more than a charismatic person. But the vision must receive a positive response as is the case in this letter. In Thessalonica, the new community is still in the initial enthusiasm of its recent conversion, and so Paul's words resonate with them. Indeed, "the variable that marks some periods as barren and some as rich in prophetic vision is the interest, the level of seeking, the responsiveness of the hearers."[38] The acceptance of Paul's perspective is partially dependent on the community and the underlying aspirations of a given people.

Paul's perception of the essence of Christian life is intimately connected to his understanding of *authority*. While it is true that in the New Testament there is little to say about authority in the church, the apostle does, in reality, exercise some kind of authority in the churches. Rather than by coercion or imposition, Paul generally persuades the Christians by his own word and example. He desires for them what is required by the gospel. In fact, he bases his authority and the legitimacy of his teaching on God and on the word of God. Paul reminds the community that he has been approved by God and entrusted with the gospel (2:4). It is God's word that the Thessalonians have heard and have accepted, God's word spoken to them by Paul (2:13). The gospel/word which they have received is powerful (1:5a). For Paul, it is this powerful word of the Lord that verifies his instructions and his theological reflections (4:2, 15-17). At this early point in his ministry, Paul aligns himself with the prophetic tradition of the Hebrew Bible. He understands his authority and his role as a missionary in terms of his possession of the word of God. However, even though

---

[38]Greenleaf, *Servant Leadership*, p. 8.

Paul's authority has divine legitimization,[39] Paul still asserts that leaders should earn the respect of their followers because of their ministry (5:13). Certainly, he would include himself in any statement which eliminates position or status as a source of esteem and consequently as a source of authority. Finally, Paul shares and delegates the authority he has received from the Lord. In sending Timothy, Paul reminds the reader that all authority carries with it certain responsibilities. Timothy is not only sent to Thessalonica but is given the responsibility to assist the community as Paul himself would have done (2:17ff).

Paul certainly has a perception of his role and of his authority that is foreign to the hierarchical or bureaucratic structures of today's church and society. Rather, it is more akin to the recent emphasis on the servant dimensions of leadership.

> A new moral principle is emerging which holds that the only authority deserving one's allegiance is that which is freely and knowingly granted by the led to the leader in response to, and in proportion to, the clearly evident servant stature of the leader. Those who choose to follow this principle... will freely respond only to individuals who are chosen as leaders because they are proven and trusted as servants.[40]

Paul is a leader with a Christian vision and with a particular understanding of authority which is lived out and tested in a variety of situations and with a diversity of people. Because of his reliance on personal *relationships* with individuals and with communities, Paul's leadership becomes

---

[39]See Gross, Vol. I, pp. 110-111, where he speaks about the legitimization of authority. It can come from power itself, perceived wisdom or goodness, divinity, or consent of the followers. Divine origin is indicated here as a possible source of legitimization of authority. This legitimization is Paul's explicit claim. He again draws on the prophetic tradition; see the prophets' accounts of their calls: Am 7:10-15; Is 6:1f; Jer 1:4-19.

[40]Greenleaf, *Servant Leadership*, p. 10.

situationally and existentially developed. The apostle's emphasis on relationships is a creative element in his own exercise of leadership which goes beyond the Hebrew prophetic tradition. The prophets emphasized universal issues such as injustice with little attention to individual situations of injustice within the community. Paul, however, finds the people as well as the situations an essential part of his work.

In order to pursue this aspect of Paul's leadership more fully, an assessment of his relationship with his co-workers is warranted. In 1 Thessalonians, Silvanus and Timothy are presented as Paul's immediate colleagues, but they are only a part of a larger group of local co-workers within the community (5:11-13). Paul's utilization of others is quite outstanding in the first century period. Indeed, his ". . . enlistment of full and part-time helpers on his missionary journeys, at times swelling to a quite substantial company of co-workers, has no parallel in the field of contemporary religious propagation."[41] In his approach to missionary work, Paul frequently distributes the responsibilities for leadership among his colleagues. While Paul assumes leadership in writing in the name of all three apostles, he also shares his responsibility by sending Timothy back to Thessalonica, and actually delegates this responsibility to him (3:2). However, Paul's relationship with Silvanus is quite different.

> After the second missionary journey Silvanus disappears completely from the group of Paul's co-workers mentioned in his letters. This is probably an indication of his independence; he was not a young assistant, converted by and chosen by Paul, but a respected colleague almost the equal of Paul himself, who after having worked for a period together with Paul chose to continue in other areas.[42]

---

[41]Banks, p. 169.

[42]Holmberg, p. 65.

This assessment could reflect positively or negatively on Paul. In a positive way, Paul could be the kind of leader who gives considerable freedom to his colleagues and challenges them to the fullest use of their gifts, experience and potential. However, on the other hand, Paul may not have the ability to work with a person of equal stature. Only the later letters will shed light on Paul's usual orientation and approach with his immediate co-workers. In 1 Thessalonians, it is definitely Paul who writes and Paul who sends. The observation has been made that "... for all he says about the co-operative nature of his work, Paul himself was not only the main influence in the group but the one around whose personal authority its activities centered."[43] What is said here about his relationship with the group, appears to be true in regard to his co-workers at this early stage in his missionary work. Paul seems to be the focal point and is recognized as such early in his career.

Paul's relationship with the Thessalonians is very good, and he rejoices at the news that Timothy brings him (3:8). If Paul's terms of endearment indicate his true feelings for the group (2:7-8, 11), then it can be said that "Paul not only gives what he has, the gospel, but what he is, himself."[44] Contemporary research indicates that "leaders are rated as more effective when they score high in both consideration and initiating structure."[45] For the Thessalonians, Paul's consideration seems to be deep and personal and the community remembers him affectionately (3:6). The apostle desires to serve these converts (3:10), and this commitment to service is the foundation of servant leadership in the current literature. Finally, Paul exhibits almost a carelessness about himself, while portraying a deep love and concern for those entrusted to his care (3:1). This selfless approach to the community is understood and appreciated at Thessalonica.

[43]Banks, p. 135.
[44]Best, p. 102.
[45]Stogdill, p. 140.

Paul utilizes his relationship with the community and the example of his dealings with his co-workers to challenge the Thessalonians to continue to assume responsibility for one another. He reminds them of his work among them (2:9), and exhorts them to apply all they learned from him to their own lives (4:1). In a concrete manner, Paul describes their roles, and in so doing places the responsibility for community growth and development within the group itself (4:18; 5:14). Paul is aware that spiritual leadership is not the responsibility of a few, but is the joy and the burden of the whole community. Leadership requires responsiveness, cooperation, and a distribution of labor, which means that followers cannot remain passive and inert. Realistically, "... groups carry out their functions best and attain their goals by having shared responsibilities for action and some delegation of authority."[46] Paul seems to operate with an awareness of these principles. However, Paul's fostering and urging of communal responsibility is intimately connected to his vision of Christian life. He is primarily interested in the group's Christian destiny (4:3a), and not their sociological development. In this regard, he knows that "those outside can criticize, flagellate, and disrupt, but only those who are inside can build. For the servant who has the capacity to be a builder, the greatest joy in this world is in the building."[47] Paul could easily describe himself and his community in these terms. In this letter, a positive relationship with the community is translated into a positive challenge for their continued growth and development.

Because of Paul's understanding of Christian life and of the *situation* of the community at Thessalonica, he tends to emphasize some basic points while addressing the issues raised by the community. In an overall assessment of the letter, Paul seems to concentrate on the call of the Christian as opposed to aspects of conversion, love rather than integrity, and unique rather than universal emphasis. This

---

[46]Hollander, p. 290.

[47]Greenleaf, *Servant Leadership*, p. 248.

approach is probably correct for a newly formed Christian community, for "what the apostle writes in his letters is precisely what one would expect a responsible pastor to write to new converts who are clearly keen but inexperienced and partly uninstructed."[48] Paul seems acutely aware that there is always "...the risk that a group which owes its existence to grace may degenerate into an all-too-natural 'in-group'."[49] Therefore, he focuses on Christian love (3:12). Because of his knowledge of the unique situation of believers in the midst of unbelievers, Paul offers instructions on the potential dangers of the pagan world (4:3b-6). Traditional themes are also used in Paul's exhortations so that the community can fully understand his challenge. In his references to the parousia, Paul demonstrates no hesitancy or doubt in his teaching but presents his ideas and his assurances regarding the end with certainty (4:17). Paul, in addressing the concerns regarding the end times, stresses the majesty of the occasion while also dealing with the anxiety and the questions of the community. His choice of this issue is situational as is his leadership response. However, Paul does even more; he "...redirects the Thessalonian community to the mainstream of Christian existence, to a life of faith, love and hope. Nothing extra is required of them, for such a life is already bound for the glorious parousia of Christ!"[50] Paul seems to have the ability to take concerns and to change them into realistic challenges for the community. Furthermore, the teaching and the admonitions are usually presented in a positive fashion (5:14-21) rather than by emphasizing the negative side. As a leader, he affirms the good in the people and then exhorts them to continue making progress (4:9-10).

Is Paul a successful leader in this letter? If so, what contributes to his *success*? Some indications are evident in the correspondence. Paul initially comes to the Thessalonians knowing that he has much to offer (2:1-2, 9). He seems

[48]Moore, p. 6.
[49]Whiteley, p. 55.
[50]Plevnik, p. 90.

to have a good concept of himself and generally "...the relationship of self-confidence to leadership (is) uniform in the positive direction."[51] Also leaders usually "...rate higher than their followers in self-confidence and self-esteem."[52] Not only is Paul confident in this letter, but the Thessalonians turn to him for direction. Perhaps, Paul has superior qualities, and so confidence in leadership exudes from his very person. In this letter, however, Paul does not appear as an unusually gifted person, and only the positive side of his personality is shown. However, it is clear that Paul's perception of himself and his apostolic role is closely associated with his vision of God's activity in him and in others. The source of his confidence seems to be on a religious level. Certainly, he is aware of potential weaknesses and failure, but it is the power of God at work that is formative of his leadership approach. Paul also affirms the community and "...gives whatever praise the facts allow him to give without being insincere."[53] Finally, he confirms the Thessalonians imitation of him in his faith and in his life (1:6).

Another dimension of Paul's success seems to emerge as a direct result of his experience as a missionary in both preaching and instructing. Frequently, experience itself enkindles a flexibility in approach and in the development of new forms of leadership. "Flexibility...is a characteristic that is consistently associated with being successful."[54] In later letters, Paul will change his views of Jewish unbelief while holding on to some consistent theological convictions. In 1 Thessalonians, he demonstrates his flexibility in sending Timothy when it is apparent that he cannot leave Athens (3:1-2) and in writing when personal proclamation of the word is impossible. Paul actually becomes a master letter writer over a relatively short span of time.

Another component of Paul's success is his ability to respond to concrete situations creatively. "Leadership is

[51]Stogdill, p. 53
[52]Stogdill, p. 53
[53]Whiteley, p. 59.
[54]Hamachek, p. 366.

most often a response to the questions and needs of people
rather than an invitation designed by an individual leader
for the supposed benefit of a community at large."[55] Paul
responds to situations and answers questions, rather than
present doctrine. However, he is ultimately guided by his
overall vision and a future goal.

Paul's personal relationship with the Christians in Thessalonica also moves him toward successful interaction.
Many studies suggest that: "followers tend to feel better
satisfied under a leader skilled in human relationships
... however, satisfaction tends to vary not only with type of
leadership, but with size and structure of the group."[56] The
human relations between Paul and the Thessalonians are
good; the group is very conducive to assess Paul positively.

There is a seriousness about Paul in his exercise of leadership and this attitude may contribute to his acceptance by
new Christians. "Paul never took his pastoral work lightly
as if he were merely issuing good advice, he counselled his
churches...with what he believed to be the word of God...as
seriously as when he first preached the gospel to them."[57] He
maintains this consistent attitude in both his personal
encounters and in his letters. Furthermore, Paul exhibits a
courage and a strength of conviction that proclaims the
gospel even in the face of opposition (2:2). He is not indifferent to the outcome of his mission (2:6-7, 19; 3:5), and is
almost too caught up in his work. However, in regard to his
ministry, the apostle anticipates problems by offering general exhortations (5:12), leaving the practical applications
to the people themselves. Paul's success certainly lies in his
person, his values, his motivations and his dedication. For
successful leaders, "...the wants and needs, the aspirations
and expectations of both leaders and followers (are important). And the genius of leadership lies in the manner in
which leaders see and act on their own and their followers'

[55] Padavano, p. 224.

[56] Stogdill, p. 330.

[57] Best. pp. 106-107

values and motivations."[58] Paul is already beginning to walk along this interactive path of leadership.

Paul's *early leadership* as seen in 1 Thessalonians, is indicative of what is fully developed in the later letters, for the exercise of leadership is a good indicator of later leadership. In this letter, Paul is personally and intimately involved with the community and his life is intimately bound together with the life of the church. Perhaps in the contemporary situation many "...have lost the understanding (of) personal involvement as an essential component of Christian leadership and (as) one of the elements which makes it distinctively Christian; it is love under another name!"[59] Paul's personal involvement fosters a deep personal understanding, builds on what he knows of their faith and of their awareness (3:10). The issues and the questions that are raised by the community can, therefore, be put into a context by Paul. For him "...the process called leadership very much depends upon the relationship between leaders and followers."[60] Even in this early letter, Paul senses that a certain kind of leadership belongs to the group and is the responsibility of the group. When Paul urges the group to assume its responsibility, it is usually in those areas which lead to the building up of the community in its Christian life. Paul affirms the community and presumes they consider themselves at the service of each other, even in difficult situations (5:14). Paul also recognizes the charisms present in the community (5:19-22), and his own deep spirituality is already evident in 1 Thessalonians.

Paul is creative in his exercise of leadership, building on his proclamation of the gospel in writing, and in utilizing thanksgiving to an extraordinary degree with this community. Not only is Paul aware of his call and role, but he also clarifies this reality for the Christians in his care. He is likewise aware of the importance of his own insights and

[58]Burns, p. 19.
[59]McKenzie, *Authority*, p. 96.
[60]Hollander, p. 285.

directives and so ensures the public reading of this letter (5:27). Paul begins to clarify his leadership role and is perceived as giving direction to the missionary work. Yet, he is primarily at the service of others. As if speaking of Paul, one commentator says: "The distinctive and unique honour of the Christian leader is to be the servant of the congregation 'over' which he is set.'[61]

Although leadership within the community at Thessalonica is still rudimentary, leadership in Paul himself is clearly religious leadership of a very high quality. He deals with issues and people from the perspective of his own Christian vision of life. His efforts are well received by his converts if not by others outside the Christian community. In this early letter, Paul's exercise of leadership holds promise for the future.

[61] Moore, p. 80.

# 2

# CONFLICT AND CONFRONTATION: THE LETTER TO THE GALATIANS

"I am astonished that you are so quickly deserting him who called you in the grace of Christ and turning to a different gospel" (Gal 1:6). Several interesting features are consistently noted about Paul's letter to the Galatians, namely, its unity of purpose, its polemical, spontaneous and violent nature, and its decisiveness regarding Pauline history. For the attentive reader, the opening chapter verifies this assessment of the entire correspondence. The different gospel (1:6-9), Paul's own gospel (1:11-12), his Jewish heritage (1:13-14), a seemingly defensive stance (1:10), and the beginnings of a Pauline justification of apostleship incorporated into a chronology (1:15-24ff)[1] set the tone and identify

---

[1]Hurd *1 Corinthians,* p. 15, briefly outlines the chronology of Paul from the Galatian text:

1:13-14 Paul persecuted the church
1:15-16 He is converted by God's grace
1:17a    Paul went to Arabia
1:18-20 After 3 years, Paul went to Jerusalem for 15 days
1:21    He journeyed to regions of Syria and Cilicia
2:1    after 14 years to Jerusalem again

the purpose and the approach of this letter. The movement of the Galatian argument is facilitated by Paul's literary and rhetorical skill. Likewise, his religious convictions and theological positions are emphatically expressed in this "...historic document which testifies to the first radical questioning of the Pauline gospel by the Christians themselves."[2] The letter to the Galatians has spark and color. It is an initial step in the clarification of the distinctions between the Jews and the believers in Jesus. In this chapter, an analysis of the situation, the interaction, and the leadership style of Paul confronts this central issue in Galatians. It is a matter of urgency as Christianity assumes its own identity in relation to its Jewish origin.

## The Situation

The letter to the Galatians is written by Paul probably while in Corinth during the third missionary journey. He addresses the "churches in Galatia" (1:2) and as is his custom, does not single out any local leaders as the recipients. While Galatia stands for a large area or a district, there is much discussion as to the exact destination of the letter.[3] It is well known that Paul founded churches in Antioch, Iconium, Derbe and Lystra located in southern Galatia. However, there is considerable dispute regarding his involvement in northern Galatia. Nowhere in this epistle does Paul refer to the peculiar and strong character of the north Galatians, but he clearly identifies the tendency of the Jewish settlers in the south Galatian cities to exert powerful religious influence. Although the discussion of destination

[2]Betz, *Galatians*, p. 28.
[3]See Kummel, *Introductions*, pp. 191-197, for a summary discussion of the South Galatian theory or "province hypothesis" and the North Galatian or "territory hypothesis," also Betz, *Galatians*, pp. 4f.; Guthrie, pp. 15f.; Bruce, pp. 3-18; and Ramsay's *Historical Commentary*. Most commentators prefer southern Galatia as the destination.

is interesting and does affect the dating of the letter, the specifics of the situation can be determined from the history of the period and the text itself. For example, the Galatian churches surely contained a nucleus of Jewish converts who are characterized by their strict observance of the law. Furthermore, the fact that members of the congregation are submitting to circumcision (5:2f) indicates the Gentile background of the Galatians Paul addresses (4:8; 6:12f). The congregation also seems to be a homogeneous unit that is able to be swayed; Paul speaks to them as such (4:8-9; 3:2-5). While the Galatian community has certainly turned from idols (4:8-10) and from their old religion (3:20; 4:6), Paul indicates that they are now "foolish" and "bewitched"(3:1). While he could understand very well that the gospel would impose suffering, their turning away from it at this point leads him to presume something irrational has happened. Thus Paul approaches the problem in terms of three groups who have a stake in the issue: the Galatians themselves, the apostolic group in Jerusalem, and the Judaizers or conflicting teachers. Finally, the Galatian congregation shares the typical Hellenistic views about the Spirit, has a disregard for ethical distinctions, a lack of concern about judgment, and a proud spiritual self-consciousness.

While the Galatian community itself is of interest, it is most enlightening to approach the letter from the perspective of the opponents. There is a notable distinction between the agitators or intruders (1:8-10; 5:12; 6:12-13) and the congregation itself (3:1-5; 4:8-16; 5:7-8). However, the theological approach to the underlying issue is dealt with in a unified and particular way by Paul. The opponents have been carefully studied and have been characterized as too clever to attack Paul himself, of Jewish origin by birth, or as Gentile Christians with Judaizing tendencies. However, whether the agitators are Jewish Christians or Gentile converts is not a matter of great importance. The fact of preaching another gospel contrary to the one Paul preaches, elicits a response of curse comparable to excommunication (1:9). Paul's gospel to the Gentiles, a gospel without the law, is

under attack by advocates of a Jewish legalism. Furthermore, their gospel made good sense to the community. This
turning away by the Galatians is a betrayal of Paul, just as
his preaching of the new gospel is perceived as a "betrayal of
Judaism" by his Jewish opponents.[4] It is important to note
that since Paul's letters are "...composed within the context
of a dialogue within Judaism," this observation is astute.[5]
Primitive Christianity emerges out of Judaism and so this
early situation of questioning and of conflict in Galatia, is
important and decisive. How Paul understands and relates
to Judaism may differ in his letters, but the Galatian opposition will always be a prime consideration for comprehend-
ing the ultimate separation.

Another aspect of the situation is Paul's relationship with
Peter and the Jerusalem church and the position of his
gospel in terms of the originating group. Paul indicates the
authenticity of his gospel by emphasizing his call, insight
and mission as a direct revelation of God (1:15-16). Then, he
speaks about his lack of dependence on Peter and Jerusalem
by stating what he did not do. "I did not go up to Jerusalem
to those who were apostles before me" (1:17). Although
Jerusalem is important in the mind of the Galatians since
the opponents relied on Jerusalem for their authority (cf.
Gal 2:4-5, 11-14; 4:25-26), Paul chooses Damascus for his
initial experience of Christian fellowship. His purpose in the
omission is a very specific on the level of the gospel, since he
quickly acknowledges a later on-going relationship (1:18f).
It is an accepted fact that Peter is for Paul a source of
tradition about Jesus, although this visit between the two
has a private character about it. On another occasion in
Jerusalem, Paul takes along Barnabas and Titus and
receives a confirmation of the gospel by the leaders of the
church (2:1-2, 9). The separate ministries to the Jews and to
the Gentiles, are acknowledged by both sides on the basis of
"theological insight."[6] The collection seals the agreement.

[4]See Hengel, *Judaism and Hellenism*, pp. 307-308.
[5]Davies, "Paul and his People Israel," p. 21.
[6]Betz, p. 99.

Peter is a recognized leader in Jerusalem during the time of Paul's first visit as a Christian (1:8) and continues to play an important role during the second visit (2:1ff). However, their relationship is not without conflict as the incident in Antioch indicates (2:11f).[7] Paul speaks of agreement and of approval by the Jerusalem church, although they "add nothing to me" (2:6). He also speaks of opposition and of conflict which indicates a rather complex relationship with the pillars of church, an important consideration for the Galatian church. In examining the situation in Galatia, it can be demonstrated that the community itself, the opponents and the churches in Jerusalem and Judea all take on importance. The issues involve these groups and it is to this discussion that the focus now turns.

## The Issues

In the letter to the Galatians there seems to be a central issue and a major question, the relationship of the Christian believers to Judaism. Paul, who describes himself as a zealous Jew and a persecutor of the church, is now faced with the task of reinterpreting the ancient traditions of his fathers (1:13-14). A deep sensitivity and a deep commitment to Judaism is reflected in his statements. As a Pharisee, he did not seem to have reasons to leave Judaism and to embrace another belief. Yet he responds to a new call and a new revelation (1:15-16). In his present vision of the gospel, the Mosaic observance has no part. The Galatians are called upon to imitate Paul in this radical approach (4:12). In many ways, Paul is contrasting two religious systems in his admonitions: circumcision on the one hand or a faith

---

[7] Hengel, *Acts*, p. 124, offers an interesting comment: "It is a strange contradiction that the clash in Antioch brought Paul into conflict with Peter, the one man in the community who as a close disciple of Jesus had probably always had a somewhat 'free' view of the Torah, and had proved this in Antioch also, through eating with Gentiles."

expressed through charity on the other (5:6; 6:14-15). The issue is clear as Paul exhorts the Galatians, for if they receive circumcision, they are bound to keep the whole law (5:3). To the Pharisaic Jew, the external ritual has significance only if he adheres to the entire Torah. For Paul, a token fulfillment in circumcision is inadequate, although the agitators think otherwise. It does appear that "...the opponents at the same time see themselves as the true heirs of the covenant and keepers of the law; and yet they stand over against Pharisaic Judaism, having dispensed with some aspects of the Jewish law."[8] Obedience to the law rather than rejection is advocated by them. However, Paul confronts the issue by stating that if circumcision and its implied obedience to the law is accepted, then "...Christ will be of no advantage to you" (5:2). Paul points out the christological and soteriological implications of submitting to circumcision. He understands Christ as freeing the believer from any of the constraints of a Jewish legalism. The Gentiles do not have to live like Jews, and Israel itself can discover the enhancement of its identity in Christ.

The judaizing problem is a new issue in Galatians and is an existential reality rather than a theoretical concept for Paul and community. However, there are some deeper implications in the situation and in the discussion. Paul is not only dealing with a movement hostile to himself, but also one that is hostile to the Jerusalem church. It appears that the Galatian churches believe that the disciples in Jerusalem preach circumcision and observance of the law. Because of this perception, Paul must deal with the misunderstandings of himself, of Jerusalem and of the nature of Christianity. For all his independence, Paul would find it inconceivable to break with the earliest community in Jerusalem,[9] and so must delicately deal with the distinctions and

---

[8]Brinsmead, p. 65; also see p. 107, where the opponents use of Abraham is discussed.

[9]See Hengel, *Acts*, p. 114; Munck, p. 134, states further that the Judaizing movement does not "...represent the original Christian conception of the church in the period from Jesus to Paul, but that it is a Gentile heresy that was possible only in the Pauline churches."

the continuity of his gospel. Harsh words are spoken by Paul in regard to circumcision and the law (3:10; 6:15), while the new creation is advocated.

The tension between what is Jewish and what is Christian is the central issue in Galatia, and the Jerusalem leaders themselves have slightly differing positions in this regard. For example, James advocates a more stringent position regarding the observance of the law than Peter. On the other hand, Peter is pictured as a more conservative figure when compared with Paul (2:11-12). This situation of opposition and of conflict between Cephas (Peter) and Paul uncovers another dimension of the issue. Peter's inconsistency and his fear is condemned because it betrays a separation of Jew and Gentile Christian rather than the unity of salvation in Christ. Peter did not abide by his theological convictions and in so doing, sways even Barnabas.[10] The Jewish issue is serious and is probably similar to what Paul himself faced in Jerusalem. However, the Antioch situation also had ramifications on the level of implications, that is, the Gentiles could be made to feel like second-class citizens because of Peter's action. Paul therefore confronts Peter, and they find themselves in a dilemma similar to that of the Galatians. The conflict can be pinpointed in the questioning of the necessity of Gentiles adhering to Jewish rituals and traditions. This dilemma also concerns the ministries of Peter and Paul. Peter's action tends to undermine the ministry of Paul to the Gentiles by leading to misunderstandings about the relationship of Jew and Gentile. This action is not helpful to the situation in Galatia where the community is turning away from the Pauline gospel.[11] In fact, the issue between Peter and Paul (2:14) is similar to the issue facing the Galatian community and must therefore be confronted.

[10]Betz, p. 110, comments, "The fact that a man like Barnabas decided against his former student and fellow worker Paul shows how difficult a question the Antioch meeting had to decide."

[11]Brinsmead, p. 136, offers a perceptive comment: "The Galatians have begun with one religion but are now seeking initiation into another - which is really the one they left when they just became Christians."

Paul in identifying the cause of the problem in an ironic and polemical way (1:6-10), describes the present state of the Galatian church. The church is in the process of shifting its allegiance and Paul places the blame on the opponents or false teachers. He sets up an antithesis of gospel/false gospel and then offers his own perpectives on the issue in the form of a well defined christology. With this christological grounding, Paul then deals with related issues of freedom, love, the flesh and life in the Spirit.

There is little doubt about the centrality of Christ in the letter to the Galatians (1:4; 2:16, 21; 6:14). In attempting to confront the false christology of the opponents, Paul rethinks the meaning of the law. He then speaks about the law of Christ and its dialogical function. Furthermore, his theological mind grapples with the place of the Gentiles in relation to the Jews, and so develops his doctrine of justification with its emphasis on faith in Christ, not justification by works of the law (2:16). Paul's understanding of Christ is the core and the essence of his theology, and his convictions regarding the significance of Christ emanate from his specific understanding of the cross (1:4; 6:14). He glories in the cross of Christ and views the position of Christ as unique in salvation history. The Galatian issue offers an appropriate opportunity for articulating his christology which clarifies the distinctions between Christian and Jew.

The issue of distinctions, circumcision and the law also triggers a challenge on the level of freedom (5:13). "For freedom Christ has set us free; stand fast therefore, and do not submit again to a yoke of slavery" (5:1). This strong admonition is centered in a theological conviction and it urges the protection of freedom by the exercise of it. In speaking of a loving service of one another, Paul is approaching freedom in Christ as a total way of life. His idea of freedom centers on love or *agapé* rather than on a moral or a legal code. In fact, Paul would go further and equate the exercise of freedom and the exercise of love. It is also true that faith must be perfected in love in order to lead to justification.

A number of passages in Galatians suggest that there is a concrete problem with the flesh in the community (5:13, 16, 17, 19; 6:12-13). However, Paul intertwines a positive teaching on ethical behavior in the text of his letter (5:22), and summarizes it by saying: "If we live by the Spirit, let us also walk by the Spirit" (5:25). The Galatians are given freedom and the Spirit through Christ. However, they have no law and no rituals to identify and to correct transgressions. It is interesting that Paul, after identifying the underlying issue in the community, makes other issues secondary in importance and utilizes them as a vehicle for positive christological and ethical teaching.[12] His prioritizing is an example of his leadership at work.

## Interaction and Response

In dealing with an issue as important as the relationship between Jews and Gentiles, Paul presents a strong foundation and a strong argument for his position. He identifies and grounds his apostolic authority, indicates his actual relationship to Peter and to the Jerusalem church, personally responds to the Galatian community and then deals concretely with the issue itself and with the opponents. Each of these areas is to be examined to identify the leadership dynamics at work.

As Paul indicates, the Galatian community is turning to a different gospel (1:6), and he perceives this conversion as an affront to the gospel he preaches. Paul is challenged to reestablish himself and his message with this community. He is on the defensive rather than in an offensive position. In reacting against the accusations implied in the letter, he

---

[12]McKenzie, *Authority*, p. 167, summarizes this teaching well: "Everywhere in the New Testament freedom is conceived as life and action; freedom is not defined as a kind of restraint. The only restraint which the New Testament places upon freedom is love, and love, far from being a restraint of freedom, is the fullness of freedom. The Christian does not act from compulsion or coercion or obligation, but because the power of the Spirit within him is a driving principle of action."

asserts his apostleship (1:1) and thereby his authority and the authenticity of his message. What is at stake is the legitimacy of the gospel and so Paul testifies to its divine origin (1:1, 11-12). It is interesting to note the connections Paul makes in his response. Apostleship is secondary to the defense of his gospel, although the two cannot be separated. The divine origin of apostleship is a guarantee of the truth of the gospel that he preaches. In his emphasis on apostleship and gospel, Paul identifies the approach he will use to resolve the dispute. He conveys his tactic in the opening sections of the letter. If fanatics and agitators are at work in Galatia in Paul's absence, then he must confront and challenge their undermining of his position. If false accusations are being made, Paul counters them by describing himself as a servant of Christ rather than as a persuader or pleaser of men (1:10). Likewise, Paul establishes that he does not vacillate in his practice and preaching but has a consistency based on his personal revelation of the truth of the gospel (1:11-12). Furthermore, he draws upon the background of the Hebrew prophets by reflecting on his call as the work of God (1:15-16). He then demonstrates how the Jewish community and the authorities accepted him and his message (1:13 - 2:10). Biographical material is used by Paul in his gospel defense and he authenticates his letter and its content again at the end of the epistle (6:11). Paul's authority is firmly established and this authority is the basis for his entire confrontation and exposition.

Paul betrays a dynamic at work in his accounts of the Jerusalem visits and his meetings with the Jewish leaders of the church (1:18-19; 2:1-2, 5-7,9). Before establishing his relationship with the church leaders, Paul emphatically states there was no connection between himself and the authorities immediately after his conversion (1:17). This comment on Paul's part is consistent with his emphasis on divine legitimacy for his proclamation of the gospel. However, he also relates how he does establish contact with Jerusalem. Paul takes the initiative for the private visit with Cephas who is probably known to the Galatian community

(1:18). The troublemakers in Galatia seem to associate their understanding of the gospel with Cephas and are citing this tradition against Paul. Paul establishes his approval by the Jerusalem leaders, including Cephas, while he maintains a special call to preach to the Gentiles (2:2, 6f). There seems to be a uniformity of feeling, a harmony and general agreement between him and Jerusalem, although some lesser differences do emerge. It is useful to our understanding of Paul's response to the difficulties in Galatia to notice that he does indicate some opposition in Jerusalem which he subsequently overcame (2:5).[13] Because of this fact, the attack on Paul is perceived by him as an attack on the Jerusalem apostles as well. He therefore defends his relationship to them shaking his opponent's position.

While there is general approval as indicated in the accounts of the visits, Paul also establishes that authority, such as Peter's, does not necessarily imply a superiority. The opposition to Peter in Antioch and Paul's anger because of Peter's implied affront to him in his territory, is an interesting situational response. Both Peter and Paul may share the same view of apostolic freedom but they certainly apply it differently. Peter seems to be acting without principle and Paul confronts and opposes the apostle to his face (2:11-14). The three encounters with Peter must be seen together to understand why Paul rejects so vehemently Peter's adaptability in Antioch. Is there an underlying issue of territory as has been indicated, or is Paul's authority now in decline because of Peter's Antioch visit? The question cannot be answered satisfactorily but Paul certainly demonstrates that respect for authority does not eliminate confrontation when issues are involved.

While earlier assessments of the epistle assume that it contains few instances of contacts with the Galatian church,

---

[13]See Betz, p. 100, who also indicates that what is said about the opponents in Jerusalem can be applied to his present opposition in Galatia; also p. 92, where Betz identifies the narrative of the conference (2:6-10) as "...one of the most intriguing, historically fascinating, and textually complicated sections of New Testament literature."

the dialogical nature of the letter is currently being examined. The church is deserting the gospel and accepting an offending theology, therefore Paul must pass judgment on his readers. He uses the apologetic letter genre in which rhetoric plays a part. There is a persuasiveness in his arguments and defense. Since the Galatians are now accepting the theology of the intruders, Paul must initiate a dialogue on the issue. He presents his arguments in an ordered fashion in the letter, moving from experience (3:1-14), scripture (3:16-4:18), the Torah (3:19-25), baptism (3:26-28), and friendship (4:12-20), to his final exhortation and ethics (5:1-6:10). Because Paul is astonished (1:6) and perplexed (4:20) at the serious situation, the letter also has a passionate character to it. The apostle defends (1:10 - 2:10), accuses (2:11-21) attacks (3:1-5), argues (3:6-14), interprets (4:21-31), and appeals to the community both tenderly (4:12-20) and sarcastically (5:12). There is no thanksgiving and no personal greetings (6:17). In fact, a literary analysis identifies a carefully constructed conditional curse on every Christian who dares to preach a different gospel (1:8-9) and a corresponding conditional blessing on those who remain loyal to the Pauline teaching (6:16). The use of metaphors (3:1, 24; 4:19; 5:1, 7, 9, 11, 15, 22; 6:7, 10, 17) conveys a diverse background and a wide range of interests, while the rhetorical questions insure a maximum impact and challenge for the readers (3:1-5, 21; 4:15-16). The dialogue is at times forced and heated; the arguments are frequently interrupted by indignant outbursts.

However, Paul is also capable of speaking tenderly to his little children with whom he is willing to work until Christ is formed in them (4:20). Attempting to move the Galatians to a higher level of understanding and to eliminate a feeling of inferiority on their part, Paul removes himself from positions of providing all the arguments. To this end he makes use of an allegory (4:21-31) so that the Galatians can perceive the truth themselves. he also compliments their progress (5:7), appeals to friendship (4:18), and praises their attitude toward him in his need (4:13-14). There is an identification with the community and an anxiety that its members exhibit a mutual friendship and confidence (4:12). Paul speaks to the Galatian community with the support of the brethren (1:2) and the Jerusalem leaders behind him. Finally, he exhorts the community on its personal and communal responsibilities (5:26; 6:1-10). The admonitions are concrete and to the point. Self-righteousness (6:1-3) and self-illusions (6:4-5) are perceived as devastating in the community, while a walking in the Spirit is advocated (5:16, 25). Paul's response to the Galatian Christians is both a powerful and a personal revelation.

The Galatian crisis forces Paul to express several latent theological themes which eventually demonstrate the total incompatibility between any Jewish observance and the practice of Christianity. Therefore, Paul and his letter to the Galatians, epitomizes the struggle between a stubborn form of Judaism and an authentic Gentile Christian approach. Once the situation and issue are identified, Paul draws out the implications of the Galatian position. If the centrality of Christ is to be maintained, then legalism, works of the law and circumcision are to no avail (2:21). Not only is faith in Christ the means of justification (2:16), but obedience is now replaced by an active love which is the distinguishing mark of the Christian and of the new creation (5:6; 6:13). For Paul, legalism is a symptom of the sin of self-centeredness associated with Adam. The members of the community, freed from this bondage, are now children of the promise (4:28), and must live accordingly, (4:6-9). Paul anticipates that his arguments which contain a variety of appeals, will be convincing for his readers. The clarity and the conviction of Paul regarding the truth of his gospel, characterizes his approach to the issue. He argues effectively from experience and from scripture presuming that he is understood by his rather sophisticated audience. Paul is also comfortable with refutation (1:8, 11-12, 15) and warning (5:21) as he confronts the Galatians.

In a very significant passage (3:28), Paul further addresses the reality of being in Christ by speaking of equality in national, social and sexual terms. This strong theological statement is a breakthrough indicating that real differences are transformed in Christ. Unity is the result of being in Christ and previously significant distinctions are irrelevant. If freedom is an important concept for the Galatians, then they are encouraged to a new freedom which actually confronts the Judaizing issue.

In regard to the opponents themselves, Paul deals with them through his interaction with the Galatian community. He sarcastically implies that the opponents' theology is not well founded (5:8). While the Judaizers are probably using some of the same persuasive methods as Paul, Paul is confident that his view will prevail. The opponents are not named, although this procedure was a matter of rule, in order not to give them further publicity. While both Paul and the opposition are moved by religious zeal, the cross of Christ is of paramount significance only to Paul (6:12). These opponents absolutely reject Paul and the gospel (1:6-9; 4:16; 6:12) and have succeeded in putting the Galatian church in a state of confusion and uncertainty. Paul's response is to present a theology of justification by faith and a christology that undermines their position. While he exhibits the sensitivity of a true Pharisee, Paul will not compromise his own interpretation of the law. Paul deals with the opponents indirectly but his gospel is clear. Once Paul realizes what is happening in Galatia, he dramatically confronts the issue and draws out its implications. He attacks but he also constructively argues and presents. The response of Paul testifies to an interaction with ideas as well as with a community, and to his ability to use a crisis situation to teach and to exhort. The dynamics of Paul's leadership are at work and can now be assessed.

## Assessment of Leadership

In attempting to assess Paul's leadership ability in a crisis situation such as Galatia, the writer examines Paul's personal qualities, his utilization of authority, situational responses, and confrontational ability. A positive and negative assessment of his leadership is offered.

If the letter to the Galatians is animated and argumentative, the author is no less so. Paul is an intensely human *person* who feels deeply. In his range of emotions, from astonishment and disappointment to the tender image of a mother giving birth, he radiates a personal sensitivity. If a leaders' openness to emotion significantly expands his or her understanding of people, then Paul should understand others well. Paul admits to perplexity (4:20), is often ironic in his statements (1:6-7), sarcastic in his response (3:1), and blunt in his assessments (2:14; 5:12, 17). There is an urgency in his tone and his letter overcomes distance and lack of physical presence. The personal qualities of Paul seem to be decisive. Do they hinder or enhance his leadership with this community? Unfortunately, only Paul's perspective is available.

The literary genre utilized by Paul suggests a carefully written piece with skillfully interwoven arguments. The arguments are strong and varied and they encompass the entire correspondence. In using the form of "apologetic speech," a dialogic component is indicated in the development of the narrative. Paul is responding to a situation and to issues raised by opponents. In his response, Paul conveys an ability to be selective on the level of issues, there is a central one, and a skill in by-passing many details while focusing on principles. Paul has a certain ability to identify problems and a decisiveness which seems to be enhanced by his strong personality.

While Paul makes use of convention in terms of literary genre, rhetorical arguments, and letter forms, he is original and creative in their usage. As a preacher, he is accustomed to persuasion and to pleading as well as to revealing his zeal and religious commitment. The homogeneous Galatian group is open to persuasion, and Paul is confident in his ability. Furthermore, Paul passes a kind judgment on the community, saying that something irrational and untoward must have happened (3:1; 5:7). Yet he warns (5:21), exhorts and rebukes them (5:1f) because a vision of Christian life is at stake. Everything is possible when Christians live in the Spirit. About this life it is said that "the Christian is asked merely to let it happen and to share in it when it happens."[14] The very exhortations to the community are the convictions and the vision of a religious leader at work. Finally, Paul affirms any good that he does see (4:13-14). Although there are only meager attempts in Galatians, the friendship units (4:12-20) indicate the personal and human dimensions of Paul.

Paul's establishment and utilization of *authority* as an apostle strengthens his position as a religious leader. Status, approbation by official leaders, or token commendations have no place in Paul. Paul's authority as a servant of Jesus Christ is divinely revealed. His theological insights are also revealed by God (1:11-16). An affront worthy of refute is any challenge on Paul's integrity or his gospel. If the community refuses to acknowledge the legitimacy of Paul's role as apostle and preacher, his influence and effectiveness is diminished. Paul also does away with ambiguity on the level of his authority and his teaching, as well as in the understanding of his relations to his opponents. His call and revelation give him a new insight and a new ability to assess a situation.

However, while Paul is extremely selective in establishing his authority from God, he also receives it from the leaders of the Jerusalem church. Furthermore, he uses the letters themselves to exert authority. While Paul's authority is threatened in Galatia he is not yet overcome. In establishing the support of the Jerusalem leaders for his gospel Paul is reinforcing his own position, a fine leadership tactic. Finally, if great leaders are seen as servants first then Paul not only uses this language in describing himself (1:10), but also encourages the community to be servants of one another, which will result in a continuity of orientation among leader and followers.

---

[14]Betz, p. 293.

In responding to the *situation* in Galatia, Paul not only skillfully identifies the main issue but develops his argument and theology to address the problem appropriately. If something irrational has happened, Paul use a rational approach to counter it. If the group has been swayed, Paul will also use persuasion for his own ends, and is confident in doing so. Paul exercises his leadership on the issues by not only speaking to the community, but also by establishing his relationship with Peter and Jerusalem, and by undermining the theology of the opponents. The unity of issue leads to a unity of theme in this letter. The problems and their ramifications are passionately confronted by Paul, In fact, he acts as if he is at his wits end (3:4), because his apostleship and his ministry is at stake.

Paul has been accused of an inconsistency in his views and of a weakening of his gospel to suit an audience. However, with further probing, commentators have identified Paul's ability to respond differently to the demands of various situations. This situational leadership response is a tremendous asset to any leader and is dependent on the leader's flexibility as well as the maturity of the group.It seems to be a quality that belongs to both Peter and Paul, although the former is challenged in Antioch when an undermining of Paul's ministry to the Gentiles and a theological consistency is in question. The situational leader can apply principles, and is creative rather than legalistic. Paul certainly advocates life without the law, provides few specific answers, but reflects creatively and deeply on the implications of believing in Jesus. Religious convictions are operative.

In presenting a radical christology, Paul responds to the ideas of the opponents. Humanness, weakness and crucifixion (3:13; 4:4-5) and unpopular ideas are proclaimed and placed within the context of a unique love of *agapé*. For Paul, the love of Christ is revealed in the cross, just as the Father's love is, and he can emphatically speak to this reality even though it will antagonize the opponents and the community. Paul's courage and conviction is apparent. Love, freedom and the cross are inseparable; there is no room for compromise. Paul offers a new perspective in this interrelatedness and also in his reflection on the new position of humankind because of Christ (3:28).[15] The Galatian situation elicits a theological and existential response from Paul. He is capable of using a crisis as a stimulus for new, creative and radical thought. He goes beyond his Jewish roots, while being sensitive to them, and clarifies the distinctiveness of Christian life and belief.

It is said that Galatians breathes *conflict* and that no other Pauline epistle is "...so completely dominated by the exigencies of *controversy.*"[16] Yet Galatians is also a very personal letter of Paul in which the ability of this leader in the midst of controversy and conflict can be assessed. The power of the opposition, the cleverness of opponents and of leaders in the early church is evident. How does Paul emerge in the dynamic of this situation?

Paul's initial response to the crisis is confrontation and anger. Galatians is the only letter in which Paul eliminates the usual thanksgiving and immediately moves to the heart of the problem. His theology is born in part from the Jewish and Gentile issues as he attempts to reconcile conflicting interpretations. However, it is an angry, brusque and pragmatic Paul who emerges in this letter as he battles an identifiable enemy. Paul carefully suppresses the names of the opponents, while drawing out the implications of their position. The confronting and defensive attitude of Paul betrays a possible personal disturbance. Barnabas, a co-worker has been misled by the skill of the opponents and this occurence must affect Paul. Perhaps, the difficulty is one of conflicting roles as much as one of conflicting theologies as Theissen's studies suggest. Interrole conflict is often the basis of power for the group which, because of it, now determine for itself directions and activities. Paul is obviously dealing with powerful opposition and a turning away from his gospel by

---

[15]Witherington, p. 593, points out that the rabbis made statements similar to Gal 3:28 but referred more to the attitude of God. Paul does the opposite in emphasizing the new position of humankind.

[16]Stanley, *Christ's Resurrection*, p. 147, for this point and the following on Galatians as a personal letter of Paul.

a sizable portion of the community. He is propelled into action and a spontaneity and urgency is seen.

In the conflict in Antioch, Paul readily contradicts an apostle by using the gospel itself as a norm for his actions. There is little sympathy for Peter who may be dealing with a mixed church for the first time. As a religious leader, Paul can go beyond persons to the ideas and the issues. Although the Antioch incident reflects this ability, Paul's personal sensitivities, indicated elsewhere, may heighten his confrontational response.

In Galatians, as in his other letters, Paul sharpens issues and confronts opposition by using antithesis. While an antithetical or dualistic approach to conflict can be effective, it presents only an either/or option. Paul does overcome this simplistic approach by constantly drawing out the implications of positions and theologies. His treatment of circumcision and the law is a good example in this letter. Paul deals with conflict and controversy with directness and strength, confidence and conviction. A passionate involvement with the issues and little respect for persons and for traditions is perceived. Paul does not shrink from controversy and he himself may even be an integral part of it because of his overpowering attitudes.

In the letter to the Galatians, Paul earns both a positive and a negative assessment of his *leadership style*. A summary of these seemingly contradictory perceptions is now offered.

Many *positive* attributes can be noted in Paul as a *leader*. When his authority and his interpretations of the gospel are threatened, he responds with force, conviction and clout. There is no repression of anxiety, but instead, a strong theological and ethical response. Paul's arguments are based on tradition, factual knowledge, interpretation and experience. A certain degree of empathy and understanding is also present. These qualities contribute to good leadership.

Paul's approach is directive as he carefully presents his theological arguments. This anticipation of a positive response by the community is feasible, because although directive, he enables the community to enter into the arguments and to draw some conclusions themselves. By focusing on his positive relationship with the Jerusalem leaders, Paul risks a negative response by the community during this time of stress. However, strong leaders assess carefully, then decisively move ahead. Strong religious leaders are bold because of deeper convictions about life and reality. Paul's fortitude seems to stem from his understanding of his new freedom in Christ. His insight into Christian life forces Paul to be hopeful (5:1f) and even radical (3:1) in his exhortations and theology. Crisis leads Paul to use his influence, persuasive ability and argumentative spirit, to clarify the issues for others. Among the traits that Harvanek attributes to a leader are strength above the ordinary, a strength of spirit which is able to persuade, to read others and then to proceed with energy, patience and hope.[17] Paul exhibits these characteristics in Galatians because of his vision of himself as an apostle of Jesus Christ.

However, if strength is an asset, there is also a *negative* side to a zealous exercise of *leadership*. Paul, by his vehement and articulate manner, can readily confront a crisis but can also threaten others. His rugged independence has been identified as the most salient feature of his character. However, it can also be a blind spot for any leader. Perhaps, Paul's assessment of Peter is an example of a myopic position. The question is raised, does Paul get beyond the personal ramifications of the issue in the Antioch incident and in the conflicting Galatian situation? Does Paul overreact to the inconsistency of Peter, and the betrayal of Barnabas and the community? Other letters may temper an assessment and serve as a corrective for a possible one-sided interpretation of Paul.[18] Is Paul flexible and accommodating or

[17]See Harvanek, pp. 32-33.

[18]See Lightfoot, pp. 13-14, where he notes that Paul continues to mention Barnabas with respect; Davies, pp. 12f., notes that a possible criticism of Paul's approach in Galatians is what leads to the conciliatory tone in Romans; Bruce, p. 42, offers a caution against a one-sided interpretation of this "most Pauline" of all Paul's letters.

inconsistent? Does he respond appropriately or react negatively? The questions are important since consistent appropriate actions are constitutive of effective long-term results.

Paul may remain a paradox of humilty and arrogance as he deals with issues, ideas and people in Galatia. However, this letter does speak to our day in identifying the dangers of legalism, and the distinctiveness of Christianity. Whether Paul was sensitive or dictatorial in his approach to this church is still open to discussion. However, the tenor of the early Christian churches was one of diversity and of dispute if they are correctly perceived as "a community of the disinherited."[19] Controversy and conflict are a part of this period and the apostle is at home in the heated discussion and debates. Even if Pauline Christianity did not subsequently prevail elsewhere, the final historical result of Galatians, which is the practical extinction of Jewish Christianity, must be noted. Paul's leadership in Galatia is probably the initial step in clarifying the distinctions between Christian and Jew. His confrontational skills lead to dramatic results which can be described as alienating or integrating, depending on the perspective.

[19]See Gager, pp. 22-23.

# 3

# DIVISION, DIVERSITY, DEFENSE: 1 and 2 CORINTHIANS

"For it has been reported to me by Chloe's people that there is quarreling among you, my brethren. What I mean is that each of you says, 'I belong to Paul,' or 'I belong to Apollos,' or ' I belong to Cephas,' or ' I belong to Christ.' Is Christ divided?" (1 Cor 1:11-13) The Corinthian letters constitute the most valuable documents for the historian of the apostolic age because of the variety of information they contain. Not only is there a great deal of fresh and exciting theological thinking, but theology is at work not only in the criticisms but also in the establishing of persons, and in the development of ideas. Contributions include a fuller under-standing of early chronology, church structure and ritual. However, the contributions are made and the balanced perspective is presented as Paul works with a most exasper-ating community. The Corinthians have a genius for misun-derstanding the founder of their Christian church,[1] and

[1]See Murphy-O'Connor, *1 Corinthians*, p. ix.

Paul must continually clarify, correct, and challenge a very strong and diverse group. In these letters, the person Paul and the apostle Paul emerge. His commitment to the community is tested, but his concern for them is always apparent. In the examination of the situation, issues and interactions in the Corinthian correspondence, the leadership of Paul is exposed. Furthermore, the scope and depth of his response is revealed. In concrete instances Paul's leadership is threatened and even attacked. The apostle's reactions are strong and often defensive. More than in any other letter of Paul, the Corinthian correspondence offers material for an evaluation of Paul's leadership effectiveness as well as its development. In approaching the letters, 1 and 2 Corinthians must of necessity be assessed separately in regard to situation, issues and interaction. Paul's leadership is distinctive and relative to the uniqueness of the moment. However, summaries and general observations are also possible. While the endeavor to understand Paul and his relationship with this church may be arduous and tedious, the journey promises to be surprisingly rewarding.

## The Situation

To uncover the richness of the Corinthian community, a study of Corinth and Paul's relationship with it is a good starting point. The letters themselves, the portrayal of the community and its people and the uniqueness of the situations that Paul addresses are likewise essential.

Corinth was a flourishing, cosmopolitan city during the apostolic age, the capital of Achaia, the center of worship of Aphrodite, and a port city. While the wickedness of the city was proverbial, the inhabitants were also intensely curious about religious questions and exhibited an independence of thought. The citizens were on the rise socially and were economically secure because of trade, banking, and governmental administration. However, only one third of the population were full citizens, others were freedmen and slaves.

It is interesting to note that the city had little continuity in its tradition at the time of its founding as a church in 49 AD, because nothing in Corinth was more than one hundred years old.[2]

Paul's relationship with Corinth is assessed from his own genuine writings and from the *Acts*. He preached the gospel there during his second journey, baptized Stephanus' household (1 Cor 1:16-17), worked at tentmaking during his eighteen month stay, and continued his ministry by visits and by letters. Paul's second visit to the community was a sorrowful one ending in disaster (2 Cor 2:1-2; 13:2), but he made plans to visit them again (2 Cor 12:14, 21). Paul's correspondence is likewise varied and interesting. He writes an early letter which is now lost (1 Cor 5:9), responds to the Corinthians' questions (1 Cor), sends a harsh letter (2 Cor 2:3-4, 9; 7:8-12) with Titus (probably 2 Cor 10 - 13), and later dispatches a letter of reconciliation (2 Cor 1:1 - 6:13; 7:2 -9:15) with the same co-worker. The Corinthian community presents difficulties for Paul, and the seeds of bitterness are sown because Paul feels betrayed by those who should commend him (2 Cor 12:11). However, Paul could add to the usual closing greetings (1 Cor 16:19-20) a sincere word of love (1 Cor 16:24) to this troublesome community. A closer examination of each of the letters follows.

1 Corinthians is quite interesting. Not only are the contents determined by the questions and communications Paul receives from the community, but the interchange can be reconstructed. This letter is a social statement, giving evidence of the communications that did exist between Paul and the community. Some of the extremes of the lost letter are avoided in 1 Corinthians as well as its excessive caution. 1 Corinthians is generally accepted as a unified letter, with any inconsistencies or breaks attributed to the circumstances of its composition. It can be divided into two major

---

[2]See Theissen, p. 99; also Kummel, *Introduction*, p. 199, where he notes that ancient Corinth was destroyed in 146 BC, and the city was refounded by Caesar as a Roman colony; and Murphy-O'Connor, *St. Paul's Corinth*, deals throuthly with the topic.

sections consisting of news or oral reports (1:10- 6:20) and responses to a letter received by Paul (7:1 - 16:4). While there is no christological error in Corinth, the letter discusses wisdom and resurrection as well as apostleship and the pattern of Christian life. The latter subjects are fully developed in 2 Corinthians.

The discussion surrounding 2 Corinthians is again interesting but divergent. While most commentators agree on a difference in tone between chapters 10-13 and the earlier parts of the letter, there is less consensus on the reasons accounting for the differences.[3] These attempts at explanation vary from the manner of composition to theories on the composite nature of 2 Corinthians. For the purposes of this study, the writer follows the consensus of modern scholarship: 2 Corinthians 10-13 is considered the third letter of Paul and 2 Corinthians 1-9 the fourth. Without question, chapters 10-13 are harsh, defensive and impassioned, while the earlier chapters, consisting of long digressions and instructions, are aimed at preventing further misunderstanding between Paul and the community. All the surviving Corinthian correspondence lies close together in time and so changes are often quite dramatic and spontaneous. The composition of these letters as well as recent sociological studies force the reader and the scholar to think about the text in new ways. The sociological perspectives add to the situational significance of the letters.

Early in 1 Corinthians is an explicit reference to the membership of the Christian community, indicating that "not many were wise according to worldly standards, not many were powerful, not many were of noble birth"(1:26). Theissen suggests that this passage has sociological implications[4] which he presents in fascinating terms. For example, the conflict and integration indicated in the letter can be

---

[3]See Barrett, *2 Corinthians*, pp. 13f; Hurd, *1 Corinthians*, p. 110, who compare 2 Corinthians 10-13 with 1 Corinthians and reach this conclusion; also Fallon, *2 Corinthians*, pp. 4-7, for discussion of literary problems and theories; Kummel, *Introduction*, pp. 206f., for context, occasion and unity of 2 Corinthians.

[4]See Theissen, *Social Setting*, p. 72.

understood as a sociological clash within the Christian community paralleling the sociological distinctions in society at large. In fact, the social structure of the city is reflected in the internal stratification of the Corinthian congregation. Although not many were of noble birth, some certainly enjoyed privilege and status, while the greatest numbers were among the lower classes.[5] However, Paul is not necessarily upholding an ideal of poverty in this statement. Rather, the wide range of social status and categories is used to advantage. Theissen identifies an ethos called love-patriarchalism, which takes for granted social differences but ameliorates them by placing obligations of respect and love on the part of the stronger, and subordination, fidelity and esteem on the part of the weaker.[6] This realistic solution to social stratification, emphasizing an equality before God, solidarity and brotherhood, is evident in Paul (1 Cor 7:21ff; 11:3-16). It is in this context that Paul can encourage the Corinthians, whether slaves or free, to remain in their particular state (1 Cor 7:21).

Furthermore, Paul realized the importance of energetic, influential persons for the establishment and growth of the church. He therefore baptizes Crispus, ruler of the synagogue, Gaius and Stephanus. Much of the activity in Corinth is attributed to the small number of higher status persons. These Corinthians are able to travel and can further the missionary endeavor.[7] Because of the Greek

---

[5]Murphy-O'Connor, *1 Corinthians*, p. 16, sees the greatest impact in the urban middle class; Theissen, *Social Setting*, p. 102, identifies the majority with the lower strata of society.

[6]See Theissen, *Social Setting*, pp. 107-108. Love-patriarchalism becomes increasingly evident in the deutero-Pauline and pastoral letters. It is contrasted to the synoptic tradition of the "itinerant charismatic beggar" referred to by Theissen on p. 11.

[7]Theissen, *Social Setting*, p. 91, states: "We come across several Corinthians on 'journeys': Aquila and Priscilla (Rom. 16:3; 1 Cor. 16:19; Acts 18:18-19); Phoebe (Rom. 16:1-2); Erastus (Acts 19:22); Stephanas with Achaicus and Fortunatus (1 Cor. 16:15-18); Chloe's people (1 Cor. 1:11). Perhaps Sosthenes (1 Cor. 1:1) should be added, if he is identical with the Corinthian synagogue ruler of the same name (Acts 18:17)"; also p. 92: "Of the 17 persons or circles or people named, we find nine engaged in travel."

environment, many in the community are Gentiles by birth, but the majority are familiar with Jewish teaching. This diverse social situation is reflected in the letters and often contributes to tension and conflict as well as enrichment. Among the co-workers in the Corinthian correspondence are colleagues, such as Titus and Timothy, and leaders in the local community of Corinth and elsewhere. Paul's relationship with these persons is identifiable in the letters. For example, Titus, who shares Paul's anxiety about the Corinthian church, is sent by him as the bearer of a severe letter. Timothy, who along with Silvanus, preached in Corinth (2 Cor 1:19) is also sent (1 Cor 4:17). Brethren are likewise sent by Paul (2 Cor 8:22; 9:3, 5), and these enjoy the full power of the apostle who commissions them. These emissaries are senior to the local community leaders, and Paul urges respect and acceptance by all (2 Cor 7:14-15; 1 Cor 16:10-11). Paul himself rejoices at the work of these messengers (2 Cor 7:6-7, 13), although some may be unsuccessful.

Many other co-workers become known in these letters: Sosthenes, a former Jew at Corinth (1 Cor 1:1), Aquila and Prisca, Jewish refugees from Rome (1 Cor 16:19), Crispus, Stephanus, Fortunatus, and Achaicus (1 Cor 1:14-16; 16:15-18). The leaders belong to the establishment of the city, and their enthusiasm and their decisiveness are essential to begin any Christian community.

Although there is little or no formal Christian leadership in Corinth, the beginnings of organization may emerge from the household of Stephanus (1 Cor 16:15f). In relation to the various co-workers and colleagues, Paul can differentiate his own ministry and prioritize. Preaching is more important than baptizing for Paul (1 Cor 1:16). The co-workers themselves also possessed many gifts, like prophecy. With a preliminary understanding of the relationships and people in Corinth, a further glance at the uniqueness of 1 and 2 Corinthians will deepen the readers grasp of the Corinthian situation.

In 1 Corinthians one discovers a community struggling with early developmental problems, experiencing conflict on various levels, and living out an over-realized eschatology. Quarreling and dissention are being reported (1 Cor 1:10-11) within a group that possesses many gifts (1 Cor 1:7-8). There may be gnostic influences in Corinth and contact with the thought of Qumran. The community has little appreciation of the cross of Christ. At the time of 1 Corinthians there is probably little trace of Judaizers. These conditions are reflected in the issues which will be examined in detail.

A change in situation occurs between 1 and 2 Corinthians. The threat within the community now becomes a threat from without. This crisis affects Paul's relationship with the converts and gives rise to the writing of 2 Corinthians. A rival apostolate emerges, the opponents are challenging Paul and swaying the community, and the Judaizing influence is apparent (2 Cor 11:22). There may also be a change in eschatology between 1 and 2 Corinthians. The issues are quite different, for example, gnosis and sexual immorality are not discussed, and a changed situation must be presumed. 2 Corinthians is difficult to understand. Paul is being personally attacked, and the polemic between the congregation and its founder is intensified. These facts must be kept in mind as the issues are discussed.

## The Issues

The problems in Corinth are best understood when 1 and 2 Corinthians are examined separately. For this study, the issues, interaction and assessment are approached in this manner.

In the very practical letter that is 1 Corinthians, the disputes, difficulties and questions of the community are easily identified. Underlining the questions may be objections which are directed to Paul; he responds according to his perception of the Corinthians' degree of misunderstanding. The loose structure of the letter can be misleading, but a theological perspective does hold the issues together. The letter is Paul's response to oral reports and to questions in a prior Corinthian letter. These are examined in turn.

The reports that Paul receives from Corinth concern factions in the community (1 Cor 1:11), immorality (5:1) and abuses at the Lord's Supper (11:18). While it is impossible to identify Chloe's people who deliver the reports, the quarreling, for Paul, is characteristic of persons without Christ (1:10; 3:3-4). He must, therefore, address the issues and does so decisively.

The prime concern seems to be the issue of Christian leadership which the factions in chapters 1-4 imply. The leaders themselves, Paul, Apollos and Cephas, are the focal points of dissension, and the presence of a "Paul-group" implies opposition to the apostle himself. Although there is no personal rivalry between Paul and Apollos (3:8-9), the tendency of the Corinthian church to exalt one leader over another must be addressed. It is generally assumed that the divisions among church members are for non-theological reasons, arising primarily from the immaturity of the group (3:1; 14:20). This regression to a merely natural behavior is combatted with anger, sarcasm, affection and rhetorical exaggeration (3:1ff). As the founder of the community (4:15), Paul appeals (1:10), admonishes (4:14) and threatens the Corinthians (4:19-20). His concerns for unity always favor the communal good over an individualistic approach. "Is Christ divided? Was Paul crucified for you?" (1:13) The questions, posed in a blunt, staccato fashion, stimulate theological reflection.

The factions or bickerings are also related to certain Corinthian predispositions and preferences for eloquence, knowledge and wisdom (1:20). This tendency is attributed to their enthusiastic view of the world, which is related to the eschatological viewpoint of the group (4:8). Paul confronts their deception (3:18) because of the radical difference he perceives between the wisdom of God and the wisdom of the world (2:11-12). Christ-crucified is presented as the power and the wisdom of God (1:22-24), a foolish, harsh and irrelevant statement to the community. However, Paul does not attempt to make the gospel palatable to this audience. Paul understands the attitudes on wisdom also as a reflection of the Corinthian attitudes on ministry. Later in the letter, he will challenge this orientation.

The Corinthians misunderstand the gospel, the Christian leaders and their own position in the world. Paul must carefully correct their erroneous ideas. In part, he suggests the appropriate role of the Spirit (2:10), the correct foundation of the church in Jesus Christ (3:11), a perspective for the apostle's work (3:5, 9-10) and a model for Christian life (4:6). A secret and hidden wisdom (2:7), when rightly understood, leads to a foolishness for the sake of Christ (4:10f). Paul is deeply sincere as he attempts to orient the Corinthians to the realities of Christian life and ministry (4:11-13). If his written response is ineffective toward change, then he threatens to deal with the problem in person (4:18-20). The factions and disunity indicated in these early chapters are potentially serious problems. The overarching concern of Paul becomes quite specific in chapters 5 and 6.

The concern of Paul in 1 Corinthians is frequently the traditional sins of the Gentiles, idolatry and sexual immorality. The issue of immorality is prime in 1 Corinthians 5-6. Three situations are identified, 5:1-13; 6:1-11; 6:12-20, and each is a concrete illustration of the Corinthian conviction that physical actions do not have moral significance. In the first instance, the man living with his father's wife (5:1), the Corinthians seemed insensitive to a marriage forbidden by both Jewish and Roman law. Paul cannot act directly and so he offers a remedy: expel the offender (5:2-4a).[8] The apostle's concern is to convince the church that commitment is made real in the sphere of the body. Paul knows his own mind in this conflict situation; he judges the incestuous man and decides that the offender cannot be tolerated (5:3, 13). However, the community must assemble to carry out its judgment (5:4b-5), indicating shared responsibility and possibly the value of self-determination by the community. Paul's understanding of Christian life (5:6) enters into his commands. The Corinthians fail to grasp the relationship between true freedom and authentic Christian community.

---

[8]See Murphy-O'Connor, *1 Corinthians*, pp. 39-41, for discussion of this.

They have overstepped the bounds of diversity in a matter offensive even to the pagans (5:15). The community now needs to reaffirm its Christian identity as it comes together as church to deal with the issue. As the situation unfolds in the letter, Paul clarifies his previous command (5:9-11) in terms of the community of faith. The non-association to be exercised by the community against an erring church member is attributed to this principle of faith and holiness.

The treatment of the following situations also reflects an ethical character and again identifies a lapse on the part of the Corinthians. Paul therefore reminds them of his assumptions (5:6; 6:2, 9, 15, 16, 19). Underlying the question of litigation is Paul's conviction that any dispute among believers should be dealt with in the community (6:5).

Paul then returns to the situation of immorality, understanding that the Corinthians did not consider sin a real possibility for themselves. A dialogue is uncovered in this section as Paul reminds and challenges them. They are not exercising freedom (6:12), but actually dehumanizing the realm of sexuality. According to Paul, the person always has a master whether it be sin, death or the Lord (6:13, 15ff). The Christians must shun immorality because they are the temples of the Holy Spirit (6:18-19). God must be glorified in their bodies (6:20).

Finally, Paul receives reports about divisions at the Lord's Supper (11:17-34) and does not commend the community for its disunity (11:17). According to Jerome Murphy-O'Connor, "The dominant characteristic of Paul's treatment of the Eucharist is its extreme realism."[9] It is a realism based in Paul's theological understanding of Eucharist. The participants in the celebration must put on Christ (Gal 3:27), for Paul, the equivalent of putting on love, if there is to be an authentic Eucharist. Likewise, Christ is really present ". . . only when the words of institution are spoken by 'Christ,' an authentic community animated by the creative saving love which alone enables humanity to

---

[9]Murphy-O'Connor, "Eucharist," p.69.

'live'."[10] In Paul, the attitude of the community is an essential component in the eucharistic celebration. Because of this understanding, unity and harmony are a necessary prerequisite for the celebration. While Paul is not unreal in his expectations (11:19), he does understand well the difficulties in Christian growth and behavior. As Paul hands on the tradition he has received from the Lord (11:23), the proclamation becomes an "actualized theology of the cross" until he comes (11:26).[11] The Corinthians are reminded of their relationship with Christ and with each other, which is deepened through the celebration. The principles of unity, presence and anticipation of fulness are foremost. Therefore, divisions and groupings are inappropriate.

When the statements on the groups at the Lord's Supper are analyzed (11:22, 34; 14:35; 16:2), Theissen's assumptions about the internal social stratification of the community are confirmed.[12] The conflict is between poor and wealthy Christians. The sacrament of unity becomes an occasion for demonstrating social differences rather than communal integration. Paul, therefore, gives simple and realistic directions to the members of the community (11:33-34) since there is no official person who seems to be responsible for creating order at the Eucharist. Further explanations will be given when Paul visits the community.

Paul thus responds with directness and dispatch to reports about factions, immorality and abuses in the communnity. However, the major portion of 1 Corinthians deals with questions addressed to Paul by the community itself. These problems similarly arise from social status (7:1-40), the pagan environment (8:1 - 11:1), and liturgical assemblies (11:2 - 14:40). Paul attempts to keep the many facets and dimensions of the problem in view as he moves through the issues.

[10]Murphy-O'Connor, "Eucharist," p.69.

[11]Bornkamm, *Paul*, p. 193.

[12]See Theissen, *Social Setting*, p.98.

"Now concerning. . . ." is the usual indicator of a Corinthian question and it occurs in regard to marriage (7:40), idol meat (8:1 -11:1), distinctions between men and women (11:2-16), spiritual gifts (12-14), the collection (16:1-4) and Apollos (16:12). "Now I would remind you. . . ." introduces the resurrection chapter (15). Each issue is now examined.

The Corinthians wrote to Paul concerning several marriage related questions (7:1). He responds to the issues by speaking to various groups and situations: the married (7:2-7, 10-12), the unmarried (7:8-9), those in mixed marriages (7:12-16) and widows (7:39-40). Paul identifies principles to govern Christian life (7:17-24) and offers three approaches to virginity (7:25-28, 29-35, 36-38). Since Paul is conditioned in his response by what the Corinthians have said, a full teaching on marriage is not presented. However, a realism characterizes the apostle's views for he realizes the tensions and the allurements of the Greek environment (7:2f). In his treatment of marriage between believers and unbelievers, Greek and Roman influences are seen in the divorce procedure (7:12f), as Paul addresses those who favor dissolution of mixed marriages (7:14). He urges reconciliation (7:10) and peace (7:15) as an appropriate response for all who are married. Furthermore, Paul elucidates a principle that everyone ought to lead the life which the Lord has assigned to him, and in which God called him (7:17).

While many factors influence Paul's views in 7:1-40, his belief that the return of the Lord was at hand is a prime consideration for interpretation as well as pastoral concern (7:26, 29). The difficult section on celibacy must be understood from this perspective as well as in terms of Paul's innate preferences (7:7-8, 32, 40). The celibacy option for women is a positive contribution of Paul,[13] and he presents it at times with a touch of humor (7:40). Finally, an understanding of gift and of holiness (7:5, 7, 14) underlies the

---

[13]See Parvey, in Ruether, *Religion and Sexism*, p. 135, where celibacy for women is seen as a radical and revolutionary choice for women. Only Christianity offers celibacy as a socially acceptable status for women during this period.

responses, traditions and teachings on marriage and related issues.

The question of food to idols (8:1f) is an emotionally charged issue, since many families, relatives and friends of the converts were non-Christian.[14] In identifying the source of the problem, Paul uses a Corinthian slogan, but accusingly characterizes the community as being "puffed up" rather than being concerned for the building up of the church (8:1). Thus, the discussion on the strong and weak, conscience and freedom, begins. The real ethical issue is freedom of conscience within the community of faith. For Paul, this freedom always implies a "freedom for" as well as a "freedom from." The ideas of the strong are presented (8:1, 4, 8, 10) as are the difficulties of the weak (8:7, 9, 11). While the identity of the weak is difficult to assess, their moral scruples, which cause friction between the groups, are identifiable. Paul would anticipate that both groups have to change. However, while he makes his own conclusions on the issue clear, Paul does not dictate a solution to the community (8:12). Rather, the apostle appeals to discernment, to common sense and to the intelligence of the strong (10:15), as well as to their awareness of the lessons of scripture (10:6). Paul focuses on their roots in Christ, communal responsibility and witness in the world (8:6, 9; 10:32-33) for the exercise of freedom of conscience. The criterion of freedom is outside of oneself (8:9; 10:31) even though the buying and eating of food in the marketplace is a neutral action (10:25). Paul urges voluntary restraint because of extenuating circumstances (10:23). The good of others is a principle and an admonition which should affect all the involved parties (10:24). Conscience formation is a concern and a contribution of Paul to the Corinthian church and to all Christians as is evidenced in this issue.

The discussion in 1 Cor 11:2-16 revolves around the distinction between men and women within the context of

---

[14]See Murphy-O'Connor, "Freedom or the Ghetto," p. 554, for a discussion of the situation affecting this issue.

the Christian assembly.[15] After a chain of originating and subordinating relationships is set up (11:3), Paul's response and arguments proceed from the order of creation (11:3, 7-12), the teaching of nature (11:13-15), and the custom of other churches (11:16). However, there is no doubt that women are equal to men in the eschatological community of faith, and that women and men should undertake liturgical leadership as the occasion arises. Reforms are indicated in the liturgy of the word and the liturgy of the Eucharist. Prayer and prophesying are not the issue, but head covering and hair length seem to consume attention. At this time, whether the head is covered or not serves as a symbol of authority or protection. Equality is preserved since both women and men are under the authority of God.

While women share fully in salvation, natural distinctions are not removed. In addition, long hair for men is associated with homosexuality by Paul and many of his contemporaries. Therefore, the seemingly trivial issues constitute acceptable behavior in the assembly. Distinctions and equality are skillfully preserved by Paul.

In Paul's development in 1 Cor 12-14 of the issue of spiritual gifts, is contained a deeper insight into community than anywhere else in the New Testament. Difficulties within the Corinthian congregation underlie this section to which Paul responds theologically and existentially. Paul's attitude of ambivalence and hostility is thinly disguised as he describes love (13:1f) in direct contrast to the Corinthians' impatience, jealousy, boastfulness, arrogance and resentfulness.

The gifts, Paul suggests, are inspired by one and the same Spirit, (12:11) and they are primarily opportunities for ser-

---

[15]There has been discussion on whether Paul is the author of these verses. Tromf, "Women in Paul," p. 198, understands the section as an interpolation, while Murphy-O'Connor, "Sex and Logic," p. 483, rejects interpolation and focuses on the discussion of women and men; however, 1 Cor 14:34-35 is seen as an interpolation by Conzelmann, *1 Corinthians* p. 246, and Murphy-O'Connor *1 Corinthians* p. 133; Munro, *Authority*, pp. 15f., and 45f., sees a later redactional stratum extending to 11:2-16 and many of the passages in subordination.

vice within the community (12:4-6). While the good of the whole regulates this use of the power of the Spirit (12:7), the individual responds consciously to make his or her contribution. However, Paul's emphasis consistently combats a privatization of faith, as he views the gifts in their sociological and communal context (14:3, 12, 26).

There is a diversity of gifts within the community and also a prioritizing of these gifts by Paul. Prophecy seems to hold a prime place for the upbuilding of the community, while apostles are the most important leaders along with the prophets and teachers (12:28). It is interesting to note that the gifts of leadership are placed in the middle of the list of other services (12:4-11) since leadership itself is not a specified ministry at this time.[16] While glossolalia is respected (14:39), it is not one of the higher gifts (12:31) which offer a maximum contribution to the church. The Corinthians would think otherwise, and Paul confronts their perception (12:4-5, 29-30; 14:13, 18-20).

According to Paul, the church is a community (12:27), bound together in unity (12:12-13, 25) and in love (13:1-13). This understanding dictates the images used by Paul and his emphasis on mutual responsibility. Because the community is the body of Christ, all meaning is derived from Christ himself, rather than simply from the utilization of gifts. This perspective is also reflected in the understanding of the functions of leadership as charisms of the Spirit rather than institutional privileges and offices. Always the ultimate criterion is the enduring quality of *agapé* or love (13:8-13). Thus, Paul addresses the issue of spiritual gifts and the Corinthian attitudes by presenting a dynamic and theological portrayal of church.

A theological reflection counters another misunderstanding in the Corinthian church, that of the resurrection of the dead (15:1-58). The error in 5:12 leads to a discussion by Paul relating the resurrection of Christ and the resurrection of Christians. A practical question is also answered (15:35)

---

[16] See Schillebeeckx, *Ministry*, p. 10.

as Paul continues a point begun in 1 Thessalonians 4:12f. Paul's perspective is christological, and the section contains an early pre-Pauline kerygmatic statement (15:3b-7). The argument proceeds from the creed; then the consequences are enumerated (15:17-18). An apocalyptic order is presented (15:23-28), and Paul makes use of Corinthian slogans (15:13, 18b) which demonstrate their disdain for the body.[17] The apostle must skillfully weave his course between a materialistic doctrine of physical resurrection and a dualistic doctrine of escape of the soul from the body. The spiritualizing of death by the Corinthians leads Paul to challenge them from the vantage of faith (15:13-19). Paul not only passes on the tradition (15:3-5), but he underlines it with his own religious convictions (15:12-21).

Paul's response to the anticipated query, "How are the dead raised? With what kind of body do they come?"(15:35), is by analogy (15:38) and by revelation of a mystery (15:51). The qualities of the risen body are enumerated (15:35-50), and Paul seems to be Pharisaic in his conception of bodily resurrection.[18] While he may diverge from strict logic in this section, Paul's concluding admonition betrays his Christian hope in a future victory (15:58). Resurrection is a central issue affecting Christian life and faith. Paul focuses on this reality in Corinthians and his later letters.

The collection is briefly spoken about by Paul to the Corinthians who probably inquired about its organization (16:1-4). While there are several statements about financial and material achievements in the letters to this church (1 Cor 16:2; 2 Cor 11:5; 1 Cor 9:1f; 2 Cor 10-13), the purpose of the Jerusalem collection is quite specific. It symbolizes the unity of the church and the equal status of its members whether they be Jew or Gentile. Paul presumes that all persons in Corinth can contribute to this endeavor, and he is

---

[17]See Murphy-O'Connor, "Slogans," p. 396.

[18]See Davies, *Paul and Judaism*, p. 306; for a discussion of the meaning of "body" and "flesh," see Bornkamm, *Paul*, pp. 130.f; Ridderbos, *Paul*, pp. 65f.; Fitzmyer, *Pauline Theology*, pp. 61f.

almost dogmatic on the practical administration of how the collection should be taken. The account indicates a lack of organization in the community, no system of finance and no collection at the worship service. Paul utilizes his experience, answers the question and provides a procedure.

Finally, Paul responds to the inquiry about Apollos and states how he urges him to visit Corinth (16:12). Consistent with his earlier designation of Apollos as a fellow-worker and servant of God (3:5, 9), Paul now refers to him as his brother. Perhaps, Paul protests too much about the lack of conflict between them, and possibly resentment does underlie this terse account. Yet, the apostle strongly urges Apollos to honor the Corinthian request for a visit. The portrayal of unity between these coworkers counters the original issue of factions addressed in this letter.

While some of the problems and questions in the Corinthian church have been complex, they are the substantive issues that stimulate the workings and dynamics of leadership. Second Corinthians provides further insight into Paul's leadership approach, and the issues are again be deduced from the correspondence.

In 2 Corinthians, attention shifts from the followers to the missionary competitors of Paul. While there is a unity of subject matter and treatment, the atmosphere and mood change sharply (1:3-4). No more is heard about food to idols and resurrection; little reference is made to gnosis and wisdom. The major issues are now the opposition to Paul, the personal attacks on him, the challenge to his apostolic authority and to his ministry. Several minor concerns and the collection also warrant examination.

A crucial question in New Testament interpretation and in the understanding of the origins of Christianity is that of opposition. The composite letter, 2 Corinthians, is overshadowed by opposition to Paul and his attempts to deal with conflicting persons and views. In an analysis of 2 Cor 10-13, three possible groups can be identified. The Corinthians themselves constitute one group for whom Paul grieves for their ingratitude and disloyalty. The other two groups are false apostles who threaten and seduce the Corinthians (11:13), and apostles of recognized eminence who are on an equal level with Paul (11:4-5). The adversaries who confront Paul by their rival apostolate are difficult specifically to identify. However, the animosity they engender probably originates from a difference in missionary style and theology (11:4) rather than a personality conflict. While these opponents are probably Jews, they are not necessarily Judaizing Jews among the Gentiles in Corinth. Whether or not two distinct groups are actually involved is inconsequential. The very existence of severe opposition is a source of embarassment to Paul. He thus characterizes the opponents as peddlers of the Word of God, avaricious and insincere (2:17). His personal pain and conflict consists in the fact that these rival apostles, instead of Paul himself, are seemingly supported by the Corinthian church. Paul is attacked personally and in respect to his authority and ministry.

The personal attacks include Paul's lack of eloquence in speech (11:16), a weak appearance (10:10), and a boldness in letters which contradict his personal presence to the community (10:1).[19] While Paul concurs that he is unskilled in speaking, he is not lacking in knowledge (11:6). He also states there is no dichotomy in his approach (10:11), defends his severe letter as a testimony of his love (2:4), a test of their obedience (2:9), and a preventive measure (2:3). Paul admits that emotionally he was experiencing anguish and affliction when he wrote to the community (2:4), and he details the afflictions he suffers (1:8-10; 6:4f). A very human plea for openness and support intertwines Paul's personal defense (7:2, 8-9).

Paul is also attacked for a fickleness or uncertainty regarding his plans to visit Corinth, and he explains his

---

[19]The unimpressive but still captivating personal appearance of Paul has frequently been noted. The often quoted *Acts of Paul and Thecla* describe him in this way: "And he saw Paul coming, a man little of stature, thin hair upon his head, crooked in the legs, of good state of body, with eyebrows joining and a nose somewhat crooked, full of grace: for sometimes he appeared like a man, and sometimes he had the face of an angel."

position (1:23; 12:14), demonstrating that the good of the community is always his motivation. Finally, Paul was previously accused of rejecting a prerogative by not accepting financial support from the Corinthian church (1 Cor 9:3-12). The Corinthians can draw the conclusion that they are less respected and loved by the apostle (2 Cor 11:11; 12:13, 15). While this conclusion is possible, Paul's reasons can be attributed to his missionary style which is that of a community organizer as opposed to an itinerant charismatic.[20] However, this refusal of financial support from the Corinthians may not be absolute (1 Cor 16:6-11; 2 Cor 1:16). These personal attacks on Paul elicit a variety of emotions, explanatory and defensive remarks.

When his apostolic authority is under fire, Paul reacts with vehemence and abruptness (10:1f). The opponents are taking credit for Paul's work of evangelization, preach a different gospel (11:4), are arrogant, tyrannical and boastful (10:12; 11:18, 20), and attach importance to their Hebrew background (11:22). These adversaries are asserting a spiritual authority and superiority (10:2), relying on visions and revelations, signs and wonders (12:12). Paul quickly challenges the Corinthians to observe what is happening (10:7) and sarcastically refers to his opponents (11:5). These apostles commend themselves (10:12), while Paul's legitimacy depends on his call (1:1) and his missionary accomplishments (10:12-18). The strength of Paul's vocation is powerful in 2 Corinthians; he has no doubts about his apostleship. When the Corinthians seek a demonstration of his apostolic authority (13:3-9), Paul urges them to test themselves. He does not acknowledge their criteria for apostolicity; rather, he portrays the true apostle in his boasts (11=12) and in his paradoxical understanding of weakness (13:9). Consistently, Paul speaks of his service and his authority for the

---

[20]See Theissen, *Social Setting*, pp. 57-58, for missionary approaches and the Corinthian conflict. He suggests two types of Christian itinerant preachers: the itinerant charismatic, a Palestinian type, characterized by poverty and community support, and a community organizer, a Hellenistic type characterized by the renunciation of support. Paul would belong to the latter group.

building up of the church (10:8; 13:10). He warns and threatens (13:2-3), defends and boasts (11:1, 30). Apostleship and ministry are closely related in his mind and in that of the opposition.

The Christian community in Corinth was the recipient of Paul's incessant labors and ministry over a long period of time. A major contributing factor to his distress in 2 Corinthians is the threat of having to admit defeat with this once flourishing church. Paul will continue to work with them (1:24), and he conveys an unshaking confidence in their response to him (3:4). His is a religious mandate (5:20; 6:1). In fact, being an "ambassador for Christ" in the "ministry of reconciliation" is a key to Paul's understanding of his work. The entire defense of his apostolate (3:1f) is a response to the accusations against him. Paul's recommendation is the Corinthian church (3:2-3), a visible sign of his apostleship. His ministry is validated not only by the Word of the gospel, but also by the fruit it bears. Therefore his apostolic authority is linked to the lived witness of the churches. An urgency and a concern is readily apparent (5:13; 6:1-3). Paul spends himself gladly (12:15) in order to regain the recognition of the Corinthians (13:6-7).

The apostle's prolonged defense (2:14 - 6:13), his eschatological perspective (5:1f), and his elaboration of the details of his ministry (6:4f), must be interpreted in light of his apostolic authority. His view of the apostolate is a direct contradiction to the perception of his opponents. Paul is aware that he can be misunderstood as he and his co-workers have already been (12:16-19). Therefore, he weaves together his argument by validating his mission (5:18), reflecting theologically on Christian life (5:17), and reinterpreting the scriptures (3:7, 18). The issues of the attacks on Paul's person, authority and ministry are interrelated in scope and content. They are addressed forcefully throughout these letters by an apostle who is at the same time committed and defensive.

Several issues are treated with dispatch. In 2 Cor 2:6-10 he mentions an individual offender in the community and suggests forgiveness and comfort. On the question of the relationship between believers and unbelievers, there is an apparent discrepancy between this passage and 1 Corinthians. Paul suggests a practical holiness, which involves a distancing from all moral defilement (7:1). Finally, the issue of the collection is addressed at length (2 Cor 8-9).

Whether 2 Corinthians 8 is a letter of recommendation for Titus or chapters 8 and 9 are written for two occasions and two audiences, the collection has theological significance and is a major activity in the churches of the 50's (Rom 15:25-32; 1 Cor 16:1-4; Gal 2:10). The unity of the church is the underlying concern of Paul as he speaks of his experiences (8:1-4; 9:1-2) and challenges the Corinthians' generosity (8:7; 9:11). While he does not pressure the church (8:8), he freely offers his advice (8:10-11; 9:13). There is also a sensitivity to the members of the community that they not be excessively burdened by their gift. Paul likewise protects himself against any implications that he would personally benefit from this aspect of his missionary work (8:20-21). Paul's persuasive campaign allows the Corinthians their freedom to decide, while offering the example of other churches as models. The apostle recommends those appointed for the task of collecting, and Titus seems to be growing in initiative and independence under Paul (8:17). While 1 and 2 Corinthians are letters of comparable length, Paul assumes a defensive stance in 2 Corinthians, and no new issues other than concrete opposition emerge.

## Interaction and Response

Within 1 and 2 Corinthians as well as in the reconstruction of Paul's lost letter and his visits, there is ample material to describe the types of interaction that occur between the founder of the church and this developing community.

The dynamics in 1 Corinthians can be described as an apostolic defense, a theological and ethical response to issues, the role of imitation, the use of tradition, the challenge of the group, and a variety of decisive actions on behalf of the congregation.

Two primary convictions seemed to govern Paul's life and go hand in hand, that Jesus is Lord and that Paul is called to be an apostle. While Paul characteristically presents himself as an apostle, in 1 Corinthians he does so as a defense of his gospel (15:1) and as a clarification of the essence of Christian life (1:1-3). If the Corinthian slogans (1:12) are best understood as declarations of independence from Paul, then the apostle skillfully reminds the community of his call (15:8-9), his effort (15:10), his status (4:15), and his skill (3:10). Paul continually asserts his apostolic authority and offers insight into the practice of authority as he deals with issues. Paul also puts into perspective other ministries (1:17) and other apostles known to the community (1:12; 9:12; 15:3-7). Paul thus uses apostleship to reestablish himself and his authority with the congregation (9:3, 8).

Furthermore, Paul identifies his apostleship in terms of his freedom in Christ (9:1-27). His utilization of freedom is a model for the church that must deal with issues such as food to idols and delicate consciences. Paul sometime sounds like an opportunist (9:19) as he rejects some of his rights and prerogatives (9:15). Is there an inconsistency, or a keen ability to accommodate and to adapt to changing circumstances? Paul also offers different criteria for apostleship than the Corinthians would present. Instead of eloquent speech, impressive gnostic theology and authoritarian behavior, he speaks of weakness, of another kind of wisdom, and of the rejection of power (1:22-24). Paul challenges the Corinthians' misunderstandings on apostleship through his reinterpretation of its requirements. Paul even uses his sufferings to advantage, as he attempts to keep the Corinthians in touch with the harsh realities of Christian life (4:11-13). Thanksgiving for their faith and an acknowledgement of their gifts (1:4, 7-8) softens an otherwise confronting defense.

Leadership appeals to motivation and makes demands as it attempts to create a unity of purpose. Paul appeals to the religious motivation of the Corinthians and their Christian principles (2:7, 10; 3:4) as he urges unity in this stratified and diverse group (1:10, 26). With their tendency to division uppermost in his mind, Paul engages in a situationally applied exercise of theology. The Body of Christ, the relational metaphors for community, his perspectives on the gifts of the Spirit, and his views on the Eucharist are examples of creative theological reflection. Furthermore, Paul exercises leadership in his directives to the Corinthian church and contributes to the theological understanding of conscience.[21] A major shift in his perception of Christ occurs in these letters and is partially a result of the Corinthians one-sided eschatological emphasis. Paul brings the cross of Christ into the forefront of his thinking. Death-resurrection is closely related to his paradoxical ideas of weakness and power which will be an ongoing concern of Paul in Corinth (1:18, 25). Within this church, death, weakness and suffering have little value. Yet Paul courageously and insightfully sees Calvary as the most expressive manifestation of *agapé* or love. In fact, herein lies the value of Christian life; all moral prescriptions are synthesized in terms of Christian love. Perhaps Paul's response to the situation in Corinth is rightly described under the headings of discernment, sense of church and love. However, a theologian at work is a fair assessment of the involvement and interaction. The Corinthians supply the issues and the questions; Paul responds with a theological depth, balance and creativity.

This theological foundation forces Paul to make ethical demands on his converts. While working through the situational difficulties, he establishes priorities and takes strong pastoral positions. In the conflict between individual freedom and its communal consequences, Paul subordinates a person's freedom to the unity of the congregation. Real ethical problems and questions are addressed on an interpersonal level. The effect of behavior on others is the criterion of ethics for Paul (10:23). Likewise, holiness is understood in terms of behavior (7:14) that is directed by

---

[21]See Stanley, "Idealism and Realism," pp. 40-41, who also states that Paul introduces the term conscience *(syneidesis)* into Christian vocabulary.

faith and love (16:14). A guiding pastoral principle includes cooperation, sensitivity and courage. The theological convictions and ethical responses to the issues demonstrate that, according to Paul, Christians operate out of a different set of values. They are in the world, but not of it.

Related to the points already discussed is Paul's exhortation to imitate him, since he imitates Christ (4:16; 11:1). For Paul, the life of an apostle should be a reflection of Christ (4:16; 11:1). For Paul, the life of an apostle should be a reflection of Christ crucified (2:1-4) and a clear expression of true Christianity. Interestingly, the apostle does not urge the imitation of Christ himself, for he understands the need of concrete models and lived examples of Christian values.[22]

Paul perceives himself as a servant of Christ and a steward of the mysteries of God (4:1-3). He acts in a trustworthy manner and is particularly sensitive to attacks on his authority (4:4). However, he understands the nature of his apostolic charism and his gift of spiritual leadership that draws others to Christ through himself. He cajoles the Corinthians (4:10) in order to elicit a change in thinking, behavior and approach. Furthermore, Paul applies principles to himself and Apollos (4:6) so that together they can model authentic existence for and within a community. He also consistently presents himself in a positive light (10:32-33) because salvation is at stake. The focus and the reason for imitation has a theological foundation and an existential application (2:1-4).

In the major traditions that Paul passes on, the Eucharist (11:23-26) and the death and resurrection of Christ (15:3-5), he reveals his knowledge of the traditions of the primitive church regarding liturgy and the Palestinian kerygma. These traditions are received and handed on; they are eschatological and joyous; they are the first written gospel traditions. Paul makes himself independent of human authority

---

[22]See Stanley, "Idealism and Realism," p. 43. He also notes, p. 42, that the notion of imitation is found exclusively in Paul's authentic writings and a few writings influenced by Paul's thought (Eph 5:1; Heb 6:12; 13:7).

in these matters (11:23) to authenticate the gospel he preaches.

Paul respects the many traditions and customs regarding marriage, food, spiritual gifts and the Jerusalem fund. Some of his prohibitions, such as the exercise of authority by women over men, are cultural taboos or Jewish religious attitudes. Church traditions are also recalled by Paul (11:2). However, while some commands are "from the Lord" (7:10), Paul also offers his own advice (7:8, 12, 25, 40). He seems to be able to weigh the importance of traditional customs, while preserving essential creedal formulas and moral directives. Furthermore, Paul reinterprets the scriptural heritage of his people (10:1f) and applies the lessons to the contemporary situation (10:6). In this regard he is flexible in his own personal approach to his Jewish heritage (9:20; Rom 9:1f; 10:1; 11:14). Paul effectively uses tradition to suit his purpose and to build his arguments. On occasion, if the passages are truly Paul's, he recalls traditional customs to avoid conflict and to preserve the prevailing position (14:35).

As a leader, Paul needs to be aware of the disruption within the group and any fragmentation associated with the environment itself. The issues in 1 Corinthians reflect both internal and external elements of disunity. Furthermore, the Corinthian ideas evident in the issues are not necessarily wrong, but simply out of perspective. Therefore, in responding to a group that seizes upon ambiguity as an occasion for misinterpretation, Paul frequently needs to clarify his positions (5:9-11). As a technique, he often quotes from their letter to criticize their ideas (6:12-13; 10:23; 7:1; 8:1, 4, 5, 8; 11:2), citing Jesus, scripture, custom and his own commission as authorities. It seems that the more Paul is questioned or attacked, the more firmly and authoritatively he grounds his statements.

The Corinthian group is often described as aggressive, argumentative, troublesome, conceited, oversensitive, infantile, and pushy. In response to these attitudes, Paul criticizes them unsparingly (8-10; 11-14), and uses anger, sarcasm (1:12f), and irony (4:8) to confront them. His severity is tempered by a conciliatory tone (4:14f), although rebuke (3:1-3) and outright challenge of their attitudes is more frequently the case (3:18; 5:6). Paul establishes himself with the group as their apostolic founder and also as a Jew to the Jews and a Gentile to the Gentiles (9:20-21). He attempts to become acceptable to all persons on their level for the sake of salvation and the gospel (9:22-23). Is there a touch of utilitarianism in these passages? Is Paul a religious chameleon? In fact, he is neither Jew nor Gentile, although he resorts to his religious and social background as another entrée to the group. Furthermore, Paul knows his converts well enough to appeal to the intelligence of the strong (10:15) and to their power of discernment. How effective he is in his interaction is partially demonstrated in 2 Corinthians.

Finally, Paul decisively acts and facilitates group growth in his interactions in 1 Corinthians. There seems to be a regulatory dimension to the letter as Paul explicity prescribes what is expected of the community.[23] He commands (7:10, 12), urges (7:1), teaches (12:1), reminds (15:1-2), judges (7:40), offers opinions on the issues (7:8, 25) and expects them to be followed. He is dogmatic and angry (11:22) and even attacks opposing views when dealing with the resurrection. The apostle also makes demands on behalf of his co-workers in terms of recognition, obedience and financial support by the community. When serious conflicts occur, Paul does not call upon local leaders, but addresses the issues himself or threatens a visit (4:18-20; 11:33-34). Regarding the specifics of the collection, he is almost dictatorial as he specifies the procedure in detail (16:1-4).

However, Paul also facilitates a maturation and growth in the congregation, as well as responsible decision-making and mutual responsibility. Usually, the apostle allows freedom where it is compatible with faith, and independence if it

---

[23]See Grant, *Historical Introduction*, pp. 182-183, where he lists the following examples: 5:1-5, 11; 6:1,5; 6:15-19; 7:3-40; 8:10-13; 10:25-28; 11:4-5, 33; 14:27-35; 16:1-4, 15-16.

does not invalidate his power. Blind faith is not advocated by Paul, and his letters can rightly be described as consultations or apostolic interventions. All members of the community are encouraged to share their gifts and to assume their leadership roles in the church. Final decisions are often left to the group, although Paul makes known his judgments and conclusions (5:3-4; 9:15; 8:12). Apparently, Paul attaches importance to mutual, shared responsibility. After clarifying the situation, he lets them draw the conclusion for themselves (1 Cor 8). It is particularly insightful to see how Paul facilitates and encourages decision-making and discernment in others. He is persuasive, clarifies and develops the arguments, and sets the parameters. Is a real consensus reached by this method? How does the community arrive at its decision? Does their final decision concur with Paul's view? Other questions also emerge in this letter. For example, does Paul pay too much attention to detail? Is he inconsistent in his thought and action (8:10; 10:25f)? Does he tell the Corinthians what to do under subtle disguises and subterfuges? Does he respect and love the community? And finally, does Paul deal differently with the oral reports and the written questions? Some of these inquiries will be addressed in the later Corinthian correspondence.

Paul's response to opposition and to threat is severe, personal and passionate in 2 Corinthians, as he defends himself, his apostolic authority and his ministry. The apostle seems to agonize over the seduction of the church by the opponents. Likewise, his approach changes after his harsh words in 2 Cor 10-13 to a reconciling and understanding tone and demeanor in 2 Cor 1-9. Some underlying Corinthian attitudes continue to persist, and Paul is forced to boasting and to a reiteration of his understanding of the cross.

In his personal defense, Paul may not only be reacting to comments and reports, but also to an inner uncertainty, distress and regret. Paul is very much concerned about maintaining his personal authority and integrity. Therefore, he speaks of his affliction, anguish and tears (2:4) as well as his love (2:3). His reason for writing (2:9) and for not visiting (1:23) are explained as a service to the community. Paul shares his deep feelings with the Corinthians; his anguish and his despair are no secret (1:8-10). He is keenly aware of the sorrow he caused them; he is personally involved in the issues and is emotionally vulnerable to criticism. Paul almost pleads for an understanding on the part of his converts (1:11-14; 6:11-13). However, he also defends himself against wrong (7:2) and attributes his boldness to Christian hope (3:12). He uses biting sarcasm to defend his position (12:13), and continues the practice of not accepting financial support from the Corinthian church despite their protests. In his personal disclosures, he is the paradox of empathy and defensiveness as he deals with misunderstanding and conflict.

Paul the person and Paul the apostle are closely aligned. In this letter, the apostle is convinced about his role and his vocation. Yet he deals with the threats to his authority in a personal and defensive manner (10:8f; 13:10). Paul and his colleagues were hurt by the community (12:16-18). Their personal attacks undermined his authority and his ministry. He reacts by boasting relentlessly, [24] by ironically playing the fool (11:1f), and by using sarcasm (11:5, 30) to justify his apostolic approach. At times, it seems that Paul is too concerned about specific attacks (11:7-8). He is "forced into" boasting of his religious experiences in order to confound the legitimacy of his opponents (12:1f). Paul's defense of his apostolic authority is more an emotional appeal than an objective defense. He is not as meek or gentle as he purports to be (10:1) as he deals with a serious confrontation.

Furthermore, Paul seems to specify a variety of incidents that tend to undermine his authority (10:7-12, 14-16). He justifies himself and cuts down his opponents by his theological overtones. Building up the community of faith is always his prime consideration. Does Paul protest too

---

[24]See Barrett, *2 Corinthians*, p. 70, where he identifies the use of boasting root words: 2 Cor - 29; 1 Cor - 9 or 10; Rom - 8; Gal - 3; Phil - 3; 1 Th - 1.

much? Is his extensive use of boasting a sign of security or insecurity? Paul's defense extends to his work and ministry itself (3:1 - 6:10). In many ways Paul is dependent on his work for his Christian identity and integrity. In the apostle's mind, no one can teach a radically different gospel and be true to the kerygma (11:4, 13). Paul defends his integrity in preaching the gospel (1:24; 2:17) and reflects on his idea of personal responsibility for the building up of the community (5:20; 12:19). Since the Corinthians themselves are the seal of his apostleship (3:2-3; 13:6), Paul is very much concerned about their faith and their fidelity (12:15). In subtle ways, he uses them to justify his actions on their behalf (4:15) and confronts the opponents' ideas to reflect on the realities of his ministry (4:16). If boasting was Paul's response to an attack on his authority, an existential understanding of weakness and suffering is his response to attacks on his personal approach to ministry.

Paul boasts of his weakness and of the sufferings he endures as a missionary (2 Cor 11). Although Paul is pained by his own shortcomings, he never feels guilty, since weakness reveals the power of Christ. This power is effective in all the concrete circumstances of Paul's life, a conviction that emanates from his prevailing christological perspective. Apostolic existence and Christian ministry will always be characterized by weakness and problems (4:8f; 6:4f; 11:23f; 12:10f). Therefore, Paul's thought moves paradoxically between the treasure of the gospel and the earthenware vessel (4:7), just as the cross itself is power and weakness, life and death.

As a servant of God, Paul endures a harsh apostolic life (6:4-8) in which outward appearances are deceptive (6:8-10). Everything is put into the context of eternal glory (4:17-18) and Paul's theological convictions (5:14). In his defense, details are given about the sufferings and hardships. Although he may be defensive (4:13), final judgment on Paul's ministry, as well as that of the Corinthians and the opponents, belongs to Christ (5:10) and to God (5:11). Reconciliation is appropriate in the interim (5:18), and the apostle's manner does convey his willingness to be reconciled to the community (1:4; 3:3; 5:1f). In 2 Corinthians, Paul must defend himself and his life's work as an apostle. He counters attacks consistently and aggressively. His theological and scriptural convictions bolster a very personal approach.

Finally, Paul responds to specific issues in a direct and forceful manner. For example, he is vacillating in his plans to visit (1:17-18), but presents the changes in a way that compliments the Corinthian church (1:15-16). He expresses his confidence in the group (7:16) as they are challenged to deal with hurt feelings and anger (7:1f). While Paul is unhappy about the developments in Corinth (12:21), he works through his own anxiety in order to correct the relationship. Paul does pursue theological objections in 2 Cor 12:19 - 13:2, and he consistently defines Christian life by its relation to Christ. His ultimatums and threats should be interpreted in this context (13:5).

Paul rejoices at the joy of his co-workers and can affirm the community in this regard (7:13-14). However, he also reminds the Corinthians of how he expects them to receive his envoys (16:10-11). Paul admonishes them to live responsibly, but often his own interests are also at stake (6:3). While the collection does have theological significance, the apostle seems to spend too much time on this issue (2 Cor 8-9). In the interaction that can be reconstructed in 2 Corinthians, a very personal Paul is revealed. He is not above attack, criticism or challenge, and he assumes a defensive stance in regard to this opposition.

## Assessment of Leadership

In 1 and 2 Corinthians there is a broad continuity and a discernable change in Paul's leadership style. These letters are good examples of an early Christian leader at work. As the situation changes, new demands are made on the apostle. As the community reacts to his instruction, another approach is necessary. Does Paul meet the extraordinary requirements of leadership during this period of his life? To further the discussion, each letter is discussed separately and then general observations are offered.

In 1 Corinthians a *situational leadership* style is evident as Paul responds to reports and to questions concerning life in the community. Since the oral reports and written inquiries are clearly distinguishable, Paul's rejoinders can be compared. It appears that the apostle is more aroused, angry and condemnatory as he deals with the oral reports from Chloe's people (1:11f; 5:1f). He does not discuss the issues but speaks decisively with little appeal to an authority other than his own. On the contrary, when he specifically mentions the Corinthians' letter, Paul's manner is calmer and more analytical (7:1f). It is also interesting to note how Paul approaches particular situations. In 1 Corinthians 7:2f, what he says is not as important as the appropriateness of his response to the underlying questions. If Paul does operate out of a love-patriarchal perspective which transcends class distinctions by advocating mutual love and respect, then the obedience of women or slaves is understandable. However, in Christ, there is equality according to Paul, and therefore his later acknowledgement of women's liturgical role is also appropriate and compatible. In 1 Cor 11:2f. the intertwining of these dual cultural and religious perspectives is visible.

Paul establishes his authority as apostle and founder of the community and is never apologetic for his changes in opinion. He believes in the Christian's ability to discern as much as he believes in his own legitimate exercise of authority. Therefore, there are no simple solutions to the problems as Paul consistently develops his earlier teaching. The religious leader, Paul, is capable of change as well as conviction, a rare combination of essential qualities.

Furthermore, Paul's ability to assess the situation correctly is enhanced by his ability to listen and to be perceived as a servant of the community. He reminds the Corinthians of his attitudes which emanate from his theological convictions concerning Christ and the church. He calls for imitation of himself because he operates from an authentic vision of Christian life. Likewise, his sincerity is evident as he attempts to orient the Corinthian church to the realities of Christian life which include suffering and weakness (4:11f). Paul is confident in his mission, and a self-confident, persuasive leader is likely to facilitate group growth and change. While many demands are made on Paul, his thinking is clear and his directives well founded. He creates alternatives for the Corinthians as he pastorally attends to the issues presented by the group. He is skilled in modifying their weaknesses by building a theological framework for his assessments. The issues on food to idols and spiritual gifts are noteworthy examples of this approach. Paul motivates the group in terms of Christian life and Christian love. While he attempts to understand their positions, he always points to a better way. Perhaps Paul anticipates bigger problems in this church if the Corinthian questions and difficulties are not addressed satisfactorily. Through his unique missionary style, he relates to and confronts this church. He continues to be the one in authority as he deals with his co-workers and with the community itself. If there is a tension, it is the tension of faith for Paul as he applies theological principles to the existential situation.

A great deal of Paul's leadership and effort are directed towards *dealing with diversity*. There is a diversity of approaches, of roles and of life-style in this letter. Paul prioritizes gifts and responsibilities within the community in direct opposition to the Corinthians' assessment of their importance. While he speaks of equality in Christ, he does recognize the legitimacy of differences on a national, social and sexual level. Genuine diversity and social stratification are not a problem for Paul who seems able to cope with these paradoxical demands. Perhaps, Paul's gift is in this realm as he attempts to achieve an integrating pattern of relationships within the community. Unity in diversity is the normative guide for his assessment of, and mediation with, the factions and in the discussion of the pneumatic gifts. Furthermore, Paul emphasizes corporate responsibility and cautiously encourages the development of local leadership. It would seem that as a leader, Paul addresses the complex issue of diversity and offers direction and insight to the congregation. On the other hand, Paul himself is intolerant of opinions other than his own as these letters also demonstrate.

An identifiable *strategy* seems to mark Paul's dealings with the Corinthian Christians. He is keen on establishing principles for operation, principles that preserve the integrity of Christian life and freedom within the community of faith. Once the principles are established, they are applied to the situations under discussion. Although there are a variety of responses to the issues, Paul's basic understanding of Christ and church remains intact. His vision and his methods are apparent, as he gives sequential attention to the problems and the demands. Paul also uses himself as a model and scripture as an example to reinforce his teachings. He works hard at clarification and direction so that conclusions may be drawn by others for themselves. The freedom of others in Christ is thus preserved.

The leadership of Paul is also evident in his ability to establish priorities. He sets priorities for his own ministerial involvement in doing what others cannot do. Whether it be preaching, instructing or defining the parameters for decision-making and action, Paul's transcendent norm is always the gospel and the building up of the church. However, there is a danger in Paul's tendency to identify what is rightly or exclusively his area of involvement. He can be insensitive or even refuse to relinquish some key functions to his co-workers and to the leaders in the community. Even a good strategy is not without limitations.

According to some scripture commentators, Paul rarely tells people what to do.[25] Rather, he utilizes persuasion, modeling, argument and judgment to elicit a personal response and personal decisions. However, while this tactic may work with the sophisticated Corinthians who are artic-

---

[25]Murphy-O'Connor, *1 Corinthians* p. 58, makes this point regarding 1 Cor 7-14; also Schnackenburg, "Community Co-operation," p. 14, who notes the community's rights to participate in decisions.

ulate and self-assured, it may be a subtle form of coercion for the other members of the group. As the group matures, Paul will be forced to decrease his control over them and to decrease his relational interaction as well. Whether he is able and willing to let go remains to be seen.

Finally, Paul's strategy is seen in his utilization of the people with means in Corinth. Their enthusiasm, drive and commitment are necessary to initiate the fledgling community. Paul seems to appeal to persons of his own social class and background as a profile of his colleagues seems to indicate. However, he realizes the dangers of too close an identification and so addresses the majority of the community in his letter (1:26-29). He also recommends that those in the upper echelon accommodate their behavior to those in the lower classes.

Paul's *success* in 1 Corinthians is due in part to the religious justification of his life (2:1-4). He thoroughly appreciates his own personal gifts and his apostolic vocation. He has the strength of character and the resiliency to contend with criticism and misunderstanding.[26] To an achievement-oriented group, he urges a striving for excellence and mature growth. Paul's own perspective on success extends beyond the present situation to cover the span of a lifetime. Authentic Christian existence is an ongoing quest. Vigor and daring characterize the apostle at this stage of his ministry. Even when established custom wins the day, Paul's fresh theological formulations must temper any critique. If leadership implies activity, movement, getting a job done, then Paul exercises leadership in this letter to the community. While he must assess the situation through the information he receives from others, Paul is willing and able to interact with others in order to identify the major issues. Paul is reasonably accepted by the community since they actively seek his advice. He is fairly successful in his endea-

---

[26]Barrett, *1 Corinthians*, p. 101, makes an insightful observation: "If Paul had attended to all the criticism of himself and of his work made within his own churches (to go no further) he would have given up his apostolate. He was not thickskinned, but simply recognized the truth (see Rom ii, 1, 19f; xiv, 4) that man is not qualified to act as his brothers's judge."

vors since many of the issues in 1 Corinthians are absent in his later letters. However, Paul's success is tempered by the fact that the relationship between him and this church actually deteriorates in the intervening period.

If there is a veiled hostility in 1 Corinthians, there is outright opposition to Paul in 2 Corinthians. Any assessment of his leadership must take into consideration the fact that he is now *under attack*, not merely misunderstood.

The situation of being opposed by intruders and by the community constitutes a crisis for Paul. He initially responds with severity but can also adapt a conciliatory demeanor since the well-being of the community is his prime concern. Paul's authority is being questioned by those who view apostleship differently. Power and authority occur frequently in this correspondence, indicating a tension and dichotomy between the various parties. It would appear that Paul understood the seriousness of the charges addressed to him personally and as an apostle. He therefore attempts to maintain his position and the integrity of his mission.

While Paul's conception of his role is in sharp contrast to that of the opponents, he does not hide behind a facade or mystique of authority, but rather willingly and openly defends himself. However, the pressure of opposing styles of leadership and a contrary gospel evoke a defensiveness in Paul's response. He seems to be deeply affected by this outright challenge and so expands his theology of the cross and even takes to boasting. While the content of his defense may be theologically accurate, it is the defensive tone that colors the argument.

While he is no stranger to *conflict and diversity*, Paul now must deal with it in a personal manner. Perhaps many of the conflicts are related to authority. In some instances, however, Paul seems negligent in taking adequate precautions against misunderstanding (2 Cor 6:14 - 7:1). While conflict can be approached philosophically, Paul seems unable to take this stance when personally questioned. Certainly, there is still a relational interdependence between Paul and the Corinthians, but he seems unable to perceive these difficulties as an essential component in group growth. Harmony and disharmony are both prerequisites and incentives to change. Perhaps Paul is unable to deal with personal remonstrations and assaults or is ineffective in coordinating adverse segments in the community. When the issue of the collection is raised by Paul, he responds in his usual way. He uses other communities as motivational examples and calls upon the positive attitudes of the Corinthians. He is sensitive and concerned.

However, Paul's ability to empathize and to accept others, is not demonstrated throughout these letters. Rather there is anxiety and distress in his all *too personal response.* The incompatibility of ideas calls forth a reaction rather than a response. Paul's warmth and tenderness are not consistently evident. More apparent is his plea for acceptance, understanding and approval. It appears that Paul places too much importance on his work and its effectiveness so that it hampers his ability to deal objectively with the issues. It also is evident that Paul's personality is unable to cope with severe personal attacks and so he frequently resorts to inappropriate behavior.

The Corinthian community is undergoing change and development. Paul is being challenged in his *ability to change* and to facilitate a new level of growth for his followers. Paul certainly provides an atmosphere of freedom in his relation with the Corinthians. They are free to express their concerns and to explore other viewpoints. However, the community seems closer to the theology of the opponents than to Paul.[27] The apostle is called upon to modify his behavior so that the followers will again accept his leadership. He does attempt this correction in 2 Corinthians 1-9 when he utilizes reconciliation as a key to mutual understanding. It is a concern that Paul's dealings with the community do not facilitate a healthy response to his efforts. Perhaps it is Paul who reads too much into the developmental crisis in Corinth and he who places too much emphasis

---

[27]See Stogdill, p. 270, where studies, when applied to this letter, suggest that the opponents in all probability, could emerge as the new leaders.

on their exploration of ideas.

In the letters to the Corinthians, a twentieth century observer is able to assess leadership in process. Because several letters and visits are a part of the material for assessment, a development and a change can be identified. It is readily acknowledged that without Paul, this church would have succumbed to religious syncretism or paganism. Because of Paul, Christians can approach their life in the world with realism and with a strong theological foundation. The church is reminded of its responsibilities, and its members are encouraged to use their many gifts for the benefit of all. Paul demonstrates his religious convictions and addresses a variety of issues in an orderly and consistent manner. Many acknowledge Paul's difficult apostolic life as well as the difficulties among this group of Christians. Admiration for his stamina, consistency and zeal is easily justified. Paul is always concerned with serving this very spirited community and endeavors to utilize his gifts on their behalf.

However, Paul seems to be a controversial figure, both accepted and rejected, as he treads through the difficult developments in Corinth. There is little restraint on Paul's part as he responds, reacts and defends. Certainly, Paul knew the Corinthian weaknesses, and yet he is almost overcome by adversity. He finds himself needing and ready to apologize. Paul seeks feedback and affirmation from his converts. Paul spends so much time with this congregation, and history gives him mixed reviews. Some say the church in Corinth was left in disarray and rebellion by Paul, never to become an influential force in Christian life. Others see his efforts bearing fruit. Certainly Paul is a unique figure in the early Christian era, as these letters testify. His uniqueness is balanced by limitations. However, while Paul's ultimate success in Corinth is open to question, his approach can offer some insights for contemporary leaders who are plagued with some of the same attitudes and difficulties that Paul faced. The fact that he does deal with adversity, conflict and an opposition recommends him and arouses admiration.

# 4

# MATURITY AND REFINEMENT: THE LETTER TO THE ROMANS

"Now the righteousness of God has been manifested apart from the law, although the law and the prophets bear witness to it, the righteousness of God through faith in Jesus Christ for all who believe" (Rom 3:21-22). The letter to the Romans is a journey in faith and a journey through time. In reality, it is a reflection of the personal journey of Paul from Judaism to believing in Jesus. It is, even more importantly, the history of a people, Israel, from the original promise to its eschatological fulfillment. Like all journeys, the voyage through Romans presents difficulties to be faced and obstacles to be overcome. However, no other New Testament writing has affected Christian theology like Romans. In spite of disputes and diversity over interpretation, the letter is foundational for life as a Christian. In many ways, Paul reaches a new depth and a new level of universality in his thought in this epistle. Not only is there a progressive development in the theological perspective of the apostle, but there is an undeniable hope for the salvation of his own people. Romans is written by a seasoned traveler toward the end of his active missionary career. Many earlier themes are recapitulated, and a remarkable resemblance between this letter and Galatians and Corinthians is apparent. Romans is a letter which traces a personal history and salvation history in a powerful and innovative manner. A rhythm and development of thought is evident in the chapters. The journey through Romans is exciting, if difficult; rewarding, if laborious; and always challenging in its timeless revelation. The gospel continues to be "...the power of God for salvation to everyone who has faith" (1:16). Paul exercises a unique form of leadership in this letter. He understands the essence and the theological ramifications of the gospel. In Romans, he is the religious leader who synthesizes and clarifies the theological content of the faith.

## The Situation

In attempting to understand the situation which resulted in Paul's letter to the Romans, several related areas must be examined. Not only should the purpose of Romans be determined, but also its relationship to Paul's personal and apostolic life must be assessed. Likewise, a knowledge of the community and the situation in Rome is essential if the text is to be validly interpreted. However, research demonstrates that none of these questions is easily understood or answered, and scholarly opinion runs the gamut of possible alternatives and positions. The journey is exciting but wrought with difficulties.

The initial question to pursue is why did Paul write Romans and what is the origin of the epistle. Recent scholarship has articulated some interesting theories and positions.[1] In the text of the epistle, Paul is quite clear about why he writes. Romans is a letter of self-introduction to a com-

---

[1] Donfried, *The Romans Debate*, is an excellent book that includes many significant contemporary studies on the purpose of Romans. Donfried's initial article, "The Nature and Scope of the Romans Debate," offers a synopsis of the issues and perspectives; Jewett, "Impulses," discusses 20th century interests; Campbell, "Romans' Debate," synthesizes articles and positions on purpose and origin; Kummel, *Introduction,* pp. 222f., discusses authenticity, integrity and related questions.

munity that Paul will soon visit on his way to Spain (1:9-15; 15:22-28; Dodd). A theological introduction is obvious in the development of the ideas and comments. The epistle is also seen as a "Last Will and Testament," and a summary of Paul's theology written from the perspective of his earlier controversies in Corinth and Galatia (Bornkamm, Karris). In this particular view, Paul's theology transcends the situation in Rome and is treated as a general presentation. The exhortations are also interpreted as broad admonitions with little semblance to the actual community situation. Since Rome is not called a church by Paul (1:7), Klein has asserted that the community needed to be fully established on the basis of apostolic authority. Paul, in stressing his commission as apostle to the Gentiles, hopes to satisfy this need by his proposed visit. Another interesting perspective is the understanding of Romans in terms of Paul's upcoming visit to Jerusalem to present the collection (15:14f.). In this view, the situation between Jewish and Gentile Christians is the major consideration, with the actual needs of the Roman community in the background. Jervell actually calls Romans 1:18 - 11:36 the "collection speech" or the defense which Paul plans to present before the church in Jerusalem.[2] Finally, Romans is sometimes perceived as a circular letter sent not only to Rome but also to other communities such as Ephesus. Many controversies and positions are summarized in the Romans letter. In this respect, a maturing of Paul's understanding of the relationship between Christian and Jew is identified. Romans 16, a chapter which often presents difficulties for interpreters, is seen as greetings to Christians in Ephesus by Manson, Käsemann and others.

However, many scholars have recently moved toward what can be described as a situational approach to the letter to the Romans. In this view, the epistle was sent by Paul to Rome in light of the concrete situation, in the Roman community (Minear, Donfreid, Cranfield, W. Campbell, Schmithals, Wiefel). Paul not only communicates his future

[2]See Jervell, "The Letter to Jerusalem," p. 64.

plai.s to the community but addresses some difficulties such as the positions of the strong and the weak, and the relationship of Jewish and Gentile Christians. Romans reflects a tension between the groups, and Paul addresses this reality in a genuine letter. Along these lines, this epistle is viewed as an ambassadorial letter reflecting the diplomacy of the apostle in a situation of discord and conflict.[3] Paul affirms communal values by his content and style. Finally, O'Neill breaks somewhat new ground, in a little accepted position, by seeing sections of Romans written to different audiences at different times by different persons.[4] From these diverse and often mutually exclusive alternatives, the actual purpose of Romans is not an easy question to answer.

For the purpose of this study, following the broad consensus of recent opinion, Romans is examined as a letter written to the Christian community in Rome in light of the concrete situation in the congregation in the middle fifties. Likewise, the integrity of Romans is accepted so that chapter 16 will be considered integral to the original letter.[5]

On the level of structure and content, Romans is viewed from the perspective of salvation history, as a gospel summary, as a treatment of the Jew and Gentile issue epitomized in chapters 9-11, and as an articulation of the original realizations that made Paul a Christian. The climax or watershed of the letter is identified as 8:1-39 by Robinson,[6] and this chapter is frequently seen as the major structural division of the letter. An inner logic seems to determine the content and the structure of the letter, and the thought and expressions are those of Paul himself. These ideas are more or less compatible with a situational approach to the understanding of Romans and are utilized in this research.

Paul writes this letter at a turning point in his apostolic

[3] See Jewett, "Ambassadorial Letter," p. 20.

[4] See O'Neill, *Romans*, p. 11.

[5] See Kummel, *Introduction*, p. 226; and Donfried, *Debate*, p. 60, who see the evidence as most convincing in this regard. For contemporary opinion see Munck, *Paul and Salvation*, p. 198, and Manson among others previously mentioned.

[6] See Robinson, *Debate*, p. 9.

career, and some of the circumstances are reflected in the document. While eagerly anticipating his visit to Rome (1:11-12, 15), Paul informs the community that he must first journey to Jerusalem (15:25) and then will travel to Rome and subsequently to Spain (15:28). In the past, difficulties prevented the apostle from visiting Rome (15:22), and his commitment to ministry certainly allowed him little time for this journey. However, Paul is also sensitive to building on the foundations of others (15:20). At this point, however, he is eager to move west (1:13), having completed his work in the east (15:9). The visit is perceived as one of mutual encouragement in faith (1:11-12). Since Paul has never visited the Roman Christian community, the letter is a kind of introduction of the apostle and his message. The gospel will again be preached to the Romans (1:15), and a new level of faith is anticipated because of the power of Christ (10:17).

The opposition Paul encountered in Galatia and in Corinth tempers his approach and his tone in Romans. In a sense, Paul writes at leisure, under no pressure of circumstances; he has completed one phase of ministry and looks forward to the next. While Paul may have to defend his gospel in Jerusalem, this intervening period, between two major ministerial commitments, provides Paul with an opportunity to synthesize and to clarify his ideas and beliefs.

The composition of the Roman congregation strongly affects this theological reflection. For God's beloved in Rome and for their faith, Paul offers thanks (1:7-8). This community, whom he addresses, which is socially and racially mixed, is probably second in size to Jerusalem. The epistle has specific references to the Gentile Christians living in Rome (1:5, 13-15; 11:13; 15:15). However, the obvious Jewish themes and interests suggest a more heterogeneous community composed of both Jews and Gentiles. Since Paul is writing to a church which has been in existence for almost a decade, the historical circumstances shed light on the question of the composition of the community. In 49 AD Claudius expelled the Jews, and probably Jewish Christians, from Rome. The church was left in the hands of the Gentile Christians until the death of Claudius in 54 AD.

Subsequently, Nero's policies allowed the return of Jewish Christians to the city. It is conceivable that a crisis did develop. The Jewish Christians now had to relate to a church whose theology had changed in the intervening period. Likewise, the Gentile Christians were challenged to a new understanding of their faith and to an appreciation of the Jewish roots of their faith. While some would leave the question of the congregation open, the tension of this change in the composition of the group can account for the content and focus of the letter. It is also interesting to observe that Christianity came to Rome apart from Paul and independent of him.

Paul's presentation of the theme of Romans makes sense in light of the changing community. He clearly states that the gospel is the power of God for salvation to the Jew first and also to the Greek (1:16). Thus, the situation in Rome which determines the focus of the epistle is actually the relationship of Jews and Gentiles. In fact, it is the question of the continuity between Judaism and Christianity that is the deeper issue addressed by Paul. If there is an opponent in the letter, it is the Jew and his understanding of salvation. Paul, therefore, must personally rethink his own theological position in terms of the impending Jerusalem visit and the concrete situation of the Roman community.[7]Paul's theology is indeed inseparable from his missionary activity, and from his own Jewish roots (9:1-3; 11:14). In Romans, therefore, divisions and tensions are addressed by a fuller understanding of justification, faith and the law. The exhortations likewise have a realistic ring and may rightly be called the ethics of crisis. However, while the letter to the Romans deals with a concrete situation in Rome, it also addresses a universal first century dilemma. Consequently, the letter should be read on both levels. With an understanding of Paul's specific and overarching purposes in mind, the issues in Romans can be identified and examined.

[7]See Sanders, *Palestinian Judaism*, p. 487; also Campbell, "Romans III," p. 39, who emphasizes the concrete situation in Rome; Donfried, *Debate*, chapter 8, deals with false presuppositions in the study of Romans and offers some interesting perspectives; Karris, pp. 149 - 151, responds to Donfried's remarks.

## The Issues

Traditionally, the letter to the Romans is seen as an in-depth articulation of the great themes in Pauline theology. According to the recent assessment of the situation in Rome, this maturing and refinement of Paul's theological understanding receives a new impetus from the real issues he must face in the Roman church. Uppermost in his mind is the relationship between Jewish and Gentile Christians, a microcosm of the relationship between Judaism and Christianity. Romans seems to revolve around this central issue as demonstrated in the questions Paul raises in the letter (3:1-8; 6:1, 15; 7:7; 9:14, 30; 11:1, 11). Therefore, the issues to be examined in this chapter are the Jewish/Gentile relationship with justification by faith, the meaning of the law, and an understanding of sin as the necessary explications of this central concern. The very practical problem of the strong and weak is also addressed.

The relationship of the Jews and Gentiles, with a broad understanding of their historical orientations and perspectives, occupies the bulk of the Roman correspondence (1-11). In Paul's thematic statements (1:16-17; 3:21-26), this problem is given a theological framework. To the community in Rome and to all Christians, Paul's reminder that the Jews have a priority in the plan of God (1:16) simply places their relationship within the spectrum of salvation history, and respects its continuity. However, salvation is not limited in Paul's thought, but is offered to all without distinction. God shows no partiality (2:11), and Paul expresses this reality by offering criticism of the Jews. Likewise, the Gentiles are admonished for deliberately suppressing the truth (1:18-32). As Paul presents the historical situation, both Jews and Gentiles stand condemned, or all are under the power of sin and in need of salvation (1:21-22; 3:9). Freedom is historically abused by both groups (1:21-22; 2:1 - 3:20; 10:16-21).

The themes of the early chapters are reiterated in chapters 9-11, a section which can also be understood in terms of church membership. Paul becomes personally involved in the images and the ideas because of his natural bonding with the Jews (9:1; 10:1; 11:1). The rejection of the Jews and their disbelief is a real problem for Paul. So developed is this section that it has been called the real center of gravity of the epistle. Where is the failure of Israel? Is God unfaithful to his promises (9:14; 10:21)? According to Paul, God's promises remain intact (9:6-13; 11:29), but Israel pursues its own interests and rejects the salvation offered to it (9:30 - 10:21). Interestingly, Paul reflects on the biblical remnant (9:27; 11:5) and sees the failure of Israel as an opportunity for the salvation of the Gentiles (11:12). In the apostle's mind, all people are ultimately bound together in the mysterious plan of God which is now actualized by faith in Jesus (3:26; 11:25-29). Paul's desires for his people, which he expresses in Romans, is an example for the church to follow. These theological reflections, often seen as a treatise, have concrete implications in the Rome community. The issue is close to the heart of Paul himself.

Once the relationship of Jews and Gentiles is put into perspective, then the major religious themes affecting all Christians must be addressed. Justification by faith is the decisive creedal formula examined by Paul. In attempting to understand any of the themes in Romans, it is important to see them as interrelated, with their development occurring throughout the epistle.

When Paul expounds and develops his gospel, it is in terms of justification by faith alone. This formulation would resonate with the Jew for whom the law would never be seen as the means of salvation. However, Paul astonishes the reader as he speaks of the righteousness of God and the righteousness of the believer in one breath (1:17). Bornkamm notes that "the distinctive feature in his gospel is that God's righteousness is conveyed to believers."[8] Both Jew

---

[8]Bornkamm, *Paul*, p. 136; Williams, "Righteousness," pp. 241-243, summarizes the understanding of the "righteousness of God" over the last 25 years. Cranfield and Bultmann would interpret it as God's gift of righteousness; Fitzmyer, Barrett, Kummel, as God's own power or activity; Ridderbos and O'Neill as human righteousness which "counts" in God's eyes.

and Gentile are justified by God's grace as a free gift, the gift which comes to humankind through the cross of Jesus Christ (3:23-25). Furthermore, justification and the people of God are interlocking themes. Not only is salvation rooted in the depths of God (8:29-30), but all those who are called are the elect (8:33). For the diverse group of Christians in Rome, there is no distinction between Jew and Gentile on the level of faith (3:22-24).

Justification is also presented in terms of the helplessness of humankind; Christ died for the ungodly (5:8). Yet mere justice would be irrelevant in this discussion; love or *agapé* is the prime motivation for God's gift in Christ. The appropriate response for all persons is a confession of faith in Jesus as Lord (10:9), tor He is the new channel of communication with God and from God.

To further expand his ideas, Paul recalls for the Jews the story of Abraham (4:1-25) and in this account the Gentiles' religious heritage. The theme of faith predominates as the patriarch responds to the gift of grace. The original promises to Abraham are still being realized by faith not by the law (4:13). It is within this context that circumcision is to be viewed, namely, as a seal of justification by faith (4:11).

Paul also draws some connections between faith and knowledge (6:9). For him, faith presumes a knowing, conscious, directed belief. This faith is based on an awareness of what God does in Christ. Furthermore, the believer is justified by faith and baptism with every dimension of life being affected. Faith is not defined by Paul but described as "faith in. . . " and "faith that. . . " Indeed, it is a response to God, correctly identified as obedience, just as the faith of Jesus was described in this manner. Paul's treatment of justification is fully developed in Romans in terms of history and life. His understanding of the law and his concept of sin is affected by this major theological insight of God's action in and through Christ.

If Paul reinterprets justification in terms of Christ, he must do no less in regard to the law. All of the apostle's discussion of the law is from the perspective of the gospel. While the law is holy (7:12), spiritual (7:14), and a delight

(7:22); a freedom from the power of the Torah is proclaimed by Paul (6:7; 7:1, 4). The law is inferior to God's salvific action in Christ (10:4); the law's function is to make invisible sin visible so that grace may abound (3:20; 5:20). According to Paul, the law itself belongs to the old aeon, along with sin and death which have been conquered in Christ (7:1). From the perspective of Christ, the law then is powerless to give life and salvation. Since all are under the law, though in different ways, all are in need of God's gift of redemption.

In attacking the law, Paul is attacking Judaism itself. In regard to the strength and the function of the law, Paul and Judaism are diametrically opposed. It is Paul's christological gospel which leads to this radical interpretation. Since the place of Christ is primary in Paul's thought, the law itself is supplanted. The universal dimension of the gospel takes precedence and so Paul can ask what advantage has the Jew? He can also explore the true meaning of circumcision and belief (2:25-29). Furthermore, faith and works are interpreted in terms of contrast: "... the grace of God on the one hand and human achievement as the ground for justification on the other."[9] Freedom from the law for both Jew and Gentile becomes an adherence to the new law of Christ (10:4). In this new mode of existence, gift and response replace works and the law.

Finally, the Jew/Gentile issue necessitates an examination of the concept of sin. Paul's starting point is again justification by faith in Christ, which actually destroys the power of sin (6:2,7) and communicates new life to the believers. Righteousness and slavery to sin cannot exist at the same time (6:20-21). However, the tension and process of sinfulness is described by Paul in Romans 7, since inner conflict is still experienced by all persons (7:23-24). Furthermore, Paul identifies sin and the flesh (7:18-20), for humankind can fall short of the glory of God by succumbing to negative tendencies. However, while persons can choose sin and rebel against God, there is a new life revealed and made

[9]Ridderbos, *Paul* p. 179.

real in Christ. Adam, sin and death are irrevocably linked (5:12), and individual responsibility for good or evil is not obliterated. However, while Adam characterizes the beginnings of history, Christ epitomizes the end with its full potential for humankind (5:12, 14, 23; 8:3). In Christ, there is a release from the power-that enslaves, and a new life in the Spirit (8:9-13). While Paul's understanding of sin is complex, taking into consideration personal, social and world dimensions, the positive freedom and potential for life is the real power of the gospel. As Paul raises the issue of sin and draws out the implications of justification in regard to sin and the law, the Roman Christians must reflect on the power of Christ transforming their lives. This transformation will have practical consequences in regard to their Christian existence.

Paul's theology is applied to a concrete situation in the Roman community: the issue of the strong and the weak. It is reminiscent of Paul's earlier discussion with the Corinthians (1 Cor 8; 9; 10:23 - 11:1) and his directions are strikingly similar. Considerable missionary experience, as well as solid theological formulations, guide the apostle's response in Romans. The difficulty centers on the actions of believers (14:10), and the strength of their assurances about what faith allows (14:1). In a pagan environment, the issue of food is a real one (14:3, 14). However, Paul, while being sensitive to the situation and to the people involved, speaks in terms of the kingdom of God (14:17) and the upbuilding of the church (14:19). The burden of responsibility is placed on the strong (14:13, 15), and judgment is recognized as the prerogative of God (14:3, 10). Personal accountability and a decision according to conscience (14:5, 23) is the true and decisive exercise of freedom for the Christian. However, a believer is not acting in love if a brother or sister is hurt by the eating of unclean food (14:15). While Paul is personally persuaded that nothing is unclean (14:14), he will not dictate a response but carefully guide a community along the path of mutual love and communal good. Theology is applied to a situation and alternatives are presented. The burden of choice rests on the persons themselves. However, the underlying principles can be applied to a variety of problems in the New Testament and contemporary world.

The issues in the letter to the Romans are ones which reflect the growing separation between Judaism and Christianity. While an appreciation of Judaism is advocated by Paul, its obsolescence is also strikingly presented. Paul's christology, stemming from his conversion experience, reinterprets the Hebrew past, while addressing the difficulties in Rome and elsewhere. In Christ, Jew and Gentile are equal and transformed.

## Interaction and Response

While Paul's theological development is superb in the letter to the Romans, there is more than a hint of his approach to the community and of his relationship to it. Although Paul is preparing for his initial visit to this group (1:15), he writes in a similar vein as he did to the Galatians and the Corinthians. The situation is different in Rome, but the emphasis of his past letters is quite appropriately and dispassionately developed. Paul's interaction is necessarily a monologue in Romans, with no first hand information or informants. However, apostolic justification, literary techniques, christological and theological approaches can be examined. A clear perspective on Christian life with its subsequent exhortations is also identified in the letter. Finally, Paul conveys an air of diplomacy as he prepares the way for his work in Rome and Spain (15:23-24).

Paul initially describes himself as a "servant of Jesus Christ, called to be an apostle, set apart for the gospel of God" (1:1). With his credentials as a Christian and as an apostle firmly identified, Paul aligns himself with the prophetic tradition in call and in service. His ministry is to preach the gospel to all nations (1:5-6), and he has the authority to do so even in Rome. It is interesting to note that ministry in the early church always develops around "the building up of the community through preaching, admonition and leadership."[10] Paul consistently places great emphasis on preaching (10:17; 15:18-26) and is not ashamed of a gospel that confronts and confounds previously held truths (1:16). Strengthening and encouragement is on the level of faith (1:11-12), a faith that is fostered by the gospel itself. As an apostle, Paul will continue to preach (15:20), work (15:17-19), interpret (1:2; 4:1f.), appeal (12:1f.), and even suffer (8:17-19). Romans is a testimony to his effectiveness and to his planning for the future.

Another dimension of Romans is its literary superiority, especially in the utilization of argument, imagery and Old Testament passages. Paul not only has facility with ideas but also is a master of style. Extensively utilized in this letter is the rhetoric of argumentation in the significant use of the Greek diatribe. Rather than a digression, the diatribe often constitutes the real theme of the letter and its development. The question and response technique raises issues and clarifies them (chps 2 and 3). Paul has a keen ability to utilize this technique and through it to question himself and others.

Confessional formulations are also strategically placed within Romans in order to capture the attention of the reader and to legitimize what follows (1:3f.; 4:25; 8:34f.; 10:9; 14:9). In addition, Paul usually connects every article of the kerygma with a moral exhortation in Romans and other letters.

In Romans 9-11, there are a considerable number of quotations from the prophets, particularly Isaiah and Jeremiah, the psalms and the Torah. Abraham (Rom 4) and Adam (Rom 5) are major examples drawn from scripture to emphasizing Paul's theological position. Paul also presents images in pairs, such as Isaac and Jacob, Moses and Pharoah, Christ and law, pot and potter, broken branches and grafting, friends and enemies, people and remnant (Rom 9-11). These are not only dramatic and colorful, they are integral to Paul's development of ideas.

---

[10]Schillebeeckx, *Ministry*, pp. 29-30, who also says that it is striking that ministry does not develop from and around the eucharist or the liturgy.

In this letter, the apostle also relegates boasting to an attitude of a natural person independent of God. Barrett comments that "boasting and faith are mutually exclusive."[11] This is a radical change from Paul's response to the Corinthian church (2 Cor 10:13f.; 11:16f.).

Furthermore, typical lists of vices are transposed in this letter (1:29-31) addressing the customary abuses of a social, religious, sexual and personal nature. Paul also negatively assesses humankind (1:18 -3:30) in order to prepare the stage for his powerful theological statements (3:21f.). Literary approaches are consistently at the service of gospel proclamation.

Early in Romans, the apostle draws attention to the universal need for salvation. Likewise, Jews and pagans, affected by the disobedience of Adam (5:12-21), are ready for the life-giving obedience of Christ. However, Christ brings more than a recompense for sin or a balancing of the scales. Life is qualitatively superior because of God's gift in Christ.[12]

It is this qualitative difference that Paul presents in his christology. To be in Christ is to be in the Spirit (8:9). Christian life is a unique mode of existence, a union with Christ who offers a new vitality and a new power to his people. Paul's understanding of Christ is one which has practical consequences for the community. His teaching is affected by the Hebrew idea of corporate personality, in which all that is predicated of the leader can also be said of the followers. Now the ultimate criterion of righteousness and ethics is Christ. Life can no longer be the same for the believer (8:32-35). Even the figures of the past, Abraham and Moses, are understood in light of the mystery of Christ. Paul seems to draw out the implications and the consequences of Christ's death and resurrection in Romans. The centrality of Christ is certainly the cornerstone of Pauline

[11]See Barrett, *Romans*, p. 82.

[12]See Barrett, *Romans*, p. 113, who states that grace overbalances sin; Cranfield, pp. 284-288, also notes the dissimilarity between Christ and Adam.

theology, and he will leave no doubt in the minds of the Roman Christians.

Thus, Paul reinterprets traditional Old Testament themes from the perspective of God's new revelation. Righteousness is a righteousness of faith, a doctrine Paul locates historically and socially. While the advantages of Judaism (3:1-2; 9:4-5) and the goodness of the law are presented (7; 9:31-32; 13:8), it is the gospel which must now interact with and challenge each new situation. Relationships and criteria have been radically altered (8:14-15). Christians are sons, heirs, children (8:14-17); glory as well as suffering is in the anticipated future. Since the Spirit is the sign and the pledge of a new liberation in Christ Jesus (8:1-2), the law and sin can no longer be the controlling power (7:24-25). A new perspective is presented by Paul. For a Jewish and a Gentile audience, possibly for the Jerusalem community as well, Paul consistently reinterprets the major tenets of Hebrew faith in light of Christ.

Paul's view of Christian life is dynamic and distinctive. Since God's righteousness is now conveyed to believers, Christian life and activity must appropriately correspond to this new relationship. While Romans 7:14-25 may reflect the ongoing tensions of life in the world and every person's existential struggle, Romans 8 is the other side of the paradox. This new reality seems more real for the apostle as he calls believers "conquerors" (8:37), who will always be united in the love of God through Christ Jesus (8:38-39). If Christ has triumphed, so have all believers. "We know that in everything God works for good with those who love him, who are called according to his purpose" (8:28).

Paul, therefore, can offer a new definition of Christian life (8:9). Christians are persons who are directed by a source outside themselves, who are enabled by the power of the Spirit. No longer are they stifled or atrophied as persons, but the promise of future life and fullness is already begun in them (8:11, 13; 6:8). How confidently Paul speaks of the fruits of God's love and justice, the guarantee of eternal life (5:1-21), a freedom from the lordship of sin (6:1 - 7:6), the gift of the Spirit and divine sonship (8:1-17), a confidence and patience while awaiting future glory (8:18-39). Earthly live is not transcended, but it is lived in a new way (5:3-5). In the daily response of the Christian is true personal growth and holiness. Paul's religious beliefs form and direct the development of his theology of Christian life.

The Christian is initiated into this new life through baptism which is described as a dying and a rising with Christ (6:2-4). Paul probably uses primitive teaching in expressing baptism as being "baptized into his death" (6:3). This close association with Christ at the salvific moment, leads to a new risen life now and in the future (6:4). "For if we have been united with him in a death like his, we shall certainly be united with him in a resurrection like his" (6:5).[13] This union implies transformation; it is now possible for the Christian to be conformed to the pattern of Christ himself. Because of what occurs in baptism, Paul can challenge the Christian to authentic living.

The exhortations in Romans are related to Paul's theological vision of life in Christ. In many ways, Paul seems to ask the impossible, knowing that all is possible in Christ.[14] Likewise, Paul combines a sublime mysticism with a very practical asceticism in his correspondence to the community. Kerygma or proclamation of belief always has implications on a moral level. The exhortations apply to the group in Rome but also to any Christian community as it matures and develops. The hortatory comments in Romans are also to be read with Paul's experience in Corinth and elsewhere in mind (12:4). Since Paul perceives the Christian as a public person, witness and external behavior are as important as interior attitudes and motivation. The letter to the Romans reflects this emphasis.

[13]See Cranfield, pp. 306f., for the various interpretations of this text; also Florence Morgan, *United to a Death Like Christ's: Rom. 6:5a*, Unpublished Dissertation (Katholieke Universiteit: Leuven), 1982, for an extensive historical analysis.

[14]See Fitzmyer, *Pauline Theology*, pp. 63-70, for an excellent summary of Christian life and being in Christ. Bornkamm, *Paul*, p. 202, states: "Because God does everything, you, too, have everything to do."

Paul is harsh and condemnatory in his assessment of certain sins of the flesh (1:26-29; 6:12-14). Exploitation and debasement are always challenged by Paul who sees these actions as the result of a person's free choice. There is a constant fight for the Christian as he or she lives within a mortal body. However, Paul reminds the Romans that final judgment in all matters rests with the Lord (2:1, 6-8) when endurance and the pursuit of a good life will also be rewarded. The eschatological perspective is never far from the apostle's mind as he views life from the perspective of the end.

Furthermore, Paul challenges the community to be different because of its Christian commitment (12:2), to be dedicated to growth and to offer the totality of life in worship (2:1). A realistic view of self is advocated (12:3) which leads to the social ethics of Paul. While the gifts of the Spirit are reminiscent of Corinthians, Paul begins to identify the esential ministries in the church as prophets, service ministries, teachers and leaders (12:6-8). The diaconate is placed in a position second to prophets in this list, because service within the community is given a very high priority by Paul (12:13). Genuine love is the mark of the Christian (12:9-10) and Paul speaks of brotherly affection in terms of honor and respect. A note of realism marks all the exhortations as the apostle encourages harmony (12:16), peace (12:18) and goodness (12:21). The very real tendencies to revenge (12:17, 19), retaliation (12:14, 21) and self-centeredness (12:16) are explicitly relegated to inauthentic existence. Empathy, zeal and service (12:11, 15) are the genuine characteristics of Christian life. It is a quality of Paul's leadership to move a community to the heights theologically, while touching the very concrete problems of human existence in his admonitions. Paul is aware that his converts belong to various groups and must live out their existence in a world of diverse values and traditions. Therefore, they must be grounded in Christ so their religious values will predominate.

Love is always the prime virtue, a love that can embrace diversity (13:10, 18). Again the eschatological perspective

lends significance to all aspects of life (13:11). Paul again
encourages the strong to exercise their freedom cautiously
(15:1) so that the community may be built up (15:2). In this
vein, dissenters should be recognized and avoided (16:17)
because of the danger they represent. Paul probably speaks
from his own experiences in many of these admonitions. His
directness and strong advice frequently betray a personally
sensitive issue (16:17).

Furthermore, Paul advocates obedience to civil authorities (13:1), good citizenship (13:5) and payment of taxes
(13:6-7). These are included in the duties of Christian life.
Obligations must be met and Paul's exhortations reveal the
spectrum of Christian responsibilities within the community and outside of it.

Finally, in the letter to the Romans, Paul diplomatically
prepares for his visit to Rome and to Jerusalem. He introduces himself to the community personally and apostolically
(1:1; 11:1). He identifies his mission and ministry to the
Gentiles (1:5-6) and outlines his plans for the future (15:28).
Likewise, Paul's theological positions are presented to the
community and thanksgiving is offered for their well-
known faith (1:8). The apostle is eager to share faith and
fellowship with them (1:12, 15) and in his statements builds
up a sense of expectation. In Romans 16, Paul indicates that
the letter is carried to Rome by a Gentile Christian, Phoebe
(16:1f.), who is a deaconess of some social standing, wealth
and independence. Likewise, the secretary Tertius (16:22) is
known to the community. Throughout this chapter greetings are sent to persons known personally to Paul, like
Prisca and Aquila (16:3-5) or by reputation. Their standing
and occupations range from slaves (16:14-15), to the city
treasurer (16:23). Paul certainly prepares for his visit by
making contacts with persons in the community and presenting a summary of his thinking in terms of the central
issue in Rome, the Jewish and Gentile relationship.

## Assessment of Leadership

Romans is unique in that Paul is not personally known to the community, and in the level of theological insight and development of the letter. Paul's leadership is likewise distinctive in his anticipation of events and in his mature and balanced response to issues. In assessing Paul's leadership style, the person, his development, diplomacy, and attitudes are examined. Furthermore, the apostle's ability to foster responsibility in the group and his role as a facilitator is explored.

As a *person*, Paul is often a controversial figure who reacts offensively and defensively when under pressure. This reaction is the result of the indissoluble connection between his apostolic experience and theology. The letter to the Romans represents a new integration of experience and a qualitative refinement of ideas, calmly and carefully presented. Paul seems to have pondered very deeply his own experiences and insights as well as those of others. In this letter, he is more concerned about his mission to preach rather than to preach successfully. While Paul is always an organizer and a planner, he seems to have a fuller understanding of himself as an apostle, now closely related to the Greco-Roman understanding of ambassador. Because of this attitude, Paul is more peaceful in Romans (5:1) and adept at diagnosing the situation from a distance.[15] In many ways, there will always be a difference between Paul and the churches, but once this difference in life-style and mission is recognized, the ministry of each can be effective. Perhaps, in Romans, leadership is more a process than a person, as Paul creatively reinterprets the Jewish tradition for the Roman community.

While Paul expresses personal anguish in regard to his people (9:2-3), he can also address the issue of the Jews

---

[15]See Hersey and Blanchard, p. 266, who suggest that effective leaders have more than good diagnostic skills and can adapt their style to suit the situational variables.

objectively from the standpoint of history (9-11). He exhibits a vigor, persistence, venturesomeness and originality in addressing the situation of Jewish and Gentile relationships. Not only is Paul able to raise consciousness and to clarify issues for the Roman church, but he is also at an advantage in regard to his immanent visit to Jerusalem (15:26, 31). In concrete ways, Paul defines Christianity, its mission and its goals in order to preserve its integrity. By his strong christological definition of justification and its implications regarding the law and circumcision, Paul is likely to engender conflict and dissent in Jerusalem. However, he anticipates this response and prepares for it. Paul also draws upon his apostolic authority, as is his custom, for his missionary endeavors and for his theological presentation. The Roman community is apt to follow and to support Paul since they are motivated by strong religious convictions. The apostle and theologian achieve new heights in the letter to the Romans.

These new levels of insight strongly indicate a growing *maturity* in Paul as a leader. It is evidenced in the formulation of a more universal application of the gospel and an expanded theological development. Reinterpretation of the message of Jesus, not mere repetition, is a characteristic of Paul. As a converted Jew, Paul struggles with the problem of how to proclaim God's new salvific acts without at least implicitly repudiating the old ones. This dilemma has contemporary counterparts and ramifications. Perhaps, Paul's methods can offer insight. He focuses on the broad issues of humanity and of sin, not simply on Israel's call and rejection. He also speaks in paradoxes and recognizes some issues as irreconcilable. Paul is bold by his own admission (15:15-16) and satisfied with the ability of the community to understand his teaching (15:14). It would appear that Paul also has a capacity to tolerate a wide span of issues and interests, a recognized qualification of leadership. Since he is in an active but transitional phase as he writes Romans, the letter becomes an indication of the apostle's adeptness to rethink, clarify and broaden his initial concepts. Paul seems to have the intellectual fortitude and integrity closely associated with eminent leadership in its mature phase. The fact that he writes Romans, after difficulties and misunderstanding in Galatia and Corinth, is testimony to his stamina and resiliency.

Paul's approach in Romans has been described as *diplomacy* at work.[16] Not only is Paul's authoritative role clarified, but he seems to guarantee success to his apostolic mission through his contacts and content. Final greetings (16) prepare the way for the missionary and gain support for his message. The defensiveness of the earlier letters by a threatened leader, gives way to a sure, steady presentation and argument. Paul skillfully involves the reader in the logic of his argument and the questioning of his mind by the extensive use of diatribe. It is also interesting to observe the level of the conversation in Romans 1-11. Obviously, Paul thinks highly of the capability of the community to deal with difficult issues and sophisticated teaching. This approach will certainly stimulate a mutual high regard if it is not threatening to the less educated in the group.

Significant *changes* can be noted in Paul's attitude and approaches to this community. Even more important than the lack of defensiveness or antagonism noted in Corinthians and Galatians is the fact that Paul is able to change his tone and demeanor. This ability to use appropriate leadership styles and to adapt to the needs of followers is an important dimension of effective leadership. Paul also focuses on the servant dimensions of Christ and the apostle (1:1; 15:8). Perhaps, more than any other aspect, the servant is characterized by listening so that responses will be both appropriate and satisfying. Paul is attentive to the situation of Rome and the church, and seeks to serve the local and larger community. Likewise, Paul offers a beautiful prayer wish (15:13) designed to instill and to foster the element of hope in the community. Change in emotional tone, change in the understanding of his religious heritage and beliefs prepare Paul for the unique demands of leadership in the diverse situations of the world of New Testament times.

[16]See Jewett, "Ambassadorial letter," pp. 12f.

While Paul's perspective on the issues is uppermost in this letter, his views of community and his fostering of *responsibility* in others is also evident. Leadership always implies a facilitating of the gifts of others. Cognizant of this fact, Paul emphasizes gifts and responsibilities as he exhorts the community in concrete and practical ways (12:4f.). Within the exhortations are the expectations of Christian life and response. When expectations are known, responsibility is fostered. The local Christian churches are expected to make their own decisions and to direct their own development because of the knowledge they possess (12:2). However, responsibility is presumed to be a mutual responsibility, designed to preserve fellowship and to build up the community. Paul's teaching on freedom and conscience is another indication of the criteria applied to an actual situation (14:13-15; 15:15). As a leader, Paul seems to elucidate principles and to apply them in given situations. He can be directive but also foster participation on various levels.

As a *facilitator*, Paul utilizes stimulating techniques to ensure the involvement of the participants. The diatribe teases the mind into active thought and startles the imagination. Romans is filled with this rhetoric of questioning and answering, a contrived dialogue of sorts (2: 3, 4, 6, 7, 9, 10, 11). Lines of argument are developed, and the arrival at a decision is the result. It has been noted that successful leaders draw out, promote and defend shared values. Paul not only articulates mutually held Christian values but also demonstrates an appreciation of Judaism which is appropriate for the Jewish and Gentile Christians (4:1f.). As a leader, Paul builds on past experience in his historical appreciation of Adam, Moses, Abraham, sin and the law. Justification is seen as a completion of the Old Testament ideas. By drawing upon the past as preparation and as promise, Paul instills a renewed historical sense into his Gentile listeners and fosters an expanding view of life for the Jews. Issues, situations and decisions must be viewed from this broad perspective if clarity and some degree of objectivity is to be assured. Relationships are thus examined historically, and the community is caught up in the largesse of history. There is little room for threat as great vistas of engaging dialogue are portrayed.

Finally, Paul draws out the implications of his theology for Christian life. However, he does not say everything. In fact, Romans itself is not a full summary of Pauline theology, nor does it deal with every aspect of life. Rather, it facilitates thought by touching and exploring some of the more profound mysteries of existence. Romans is a journey of the mind and of the spirit. There are many possible diversions and many alternative routes, but as a leader, Paul skillfully and persistently describes the difference Christ makes. In doing so, he draws distinctions between Christians, Jews and Gentiles; distinctions which can be pondered today.

Romans is a unique fusion of religious thought and contains a unique assessment of a situation. Some of the weaknesses of a purely situational theology, such as the inadequate appreciation of transcendence, are overcome in this letter. Paul exhibits an appropriate situational leadership style prior to his personal encounter with the Roman community. In many ways, distance seems to be to his advantage as he creatively and maturely refines his thought and his theological positions. Romans continues to challenge leaders to reflect again on the meaning and quality of their personal presence. For Paul, great leadership development seems to be achieved in this period of transition and relative leisure before to his Roman visit and Jerusalem journey. Distance allows what presence does not. This aspect of the assessment of Paul's leadership may speak volumes about the person, Paul, and his ultimate success.

Thus, the journey through Romans is completed with Paul's actual journey still before him. The apostle's synthesis of such important issues as the relationship of all persons within the church and the relationship of the church to its Jewish roots is substantial and revolutionary. Paul is conditioned intellectually for the next stage in his missionary work and the Romans are prepared for their personal encounter with the Apostle of the Gentiles.

# 5

# A FINAL PERSPECTIVE: THE LETTER TO THE PHILIPPIANS

"I want you to know, brethren, that what has happened to me has really served to advance the gospel, so that it has become known throughout the whole praetorium guard and to the rest that my imprisonment is for Christ (Phil 1:12-13)." In the letter to the Philippians, a document rightly seen as the last will and testament of an incarcerated apostle,[1] a uniqueness permeates the correspondence which is reflective of the intimate relationship between Paul and the community. The letter flows like a friendly conversation between friends and partners (1:7). Although it is composed during a period of extreme anxiety, Paul conveys a joy and a confidence in the Lord (1:14, 18-19). With its component parts loosely tied together, the letter contains no formal instructions or doctrinal exposition, but is, rather, the most personal and encouraging of all the letters of Paul. Surely a deep and abiding love for this community is reflected in the apostle's words of thanksgiving and longing (1:3-5, 8). The

---

[1]See Martin, *Philippians*, p. ix, who refers to John A. Hutton's statement on the letter being Paul's last will and testament; Bornkamm, "Last Will," p. 30, sees Philippians and Philemon as the only true captivity epistles.

basis of this strong affective relationship partially lies in the fact that Philippi was the first church founded by Paul on European soil. Although his missionary activity there ended with a clash, and he was driven out of the city (Ac 16:11f.; 1 Thess 2:2), the mission marked a new and significant chapter in Paul's life. He uses an extraordinary phrase when he speaks of his apostolic activity in Macedonia: "the beginning of the gospel" (4:15), even though the apostle had been preaching in Syria and Cilicia for quite a number of years (Gal 1:21; 2:1). From this church Paul accepts financial support (4:15-16), another mark of distinction. It appears that when the community was put to the test of existing on its own, it fared well, for little suggests the dangers of false doctrine in this New Testament epistle.

Philippians is a letter written by someone suffering for his religious convictions and for his ministry as an apostle of Christ. In an examination of the situation, issues and interaction, the attitudes, emphases and motivations of an imprisoned leader emerge. As Paul exercises his leadership under the threat of death (2:17), the quality and caliber of his apostolic life and thought becomes increasingly more apparent.

## The Situation

The fascinating situation underlying Paul's letter to the Philippians is illuminated by a study of the background and composition of the community, the apostle's initial and ongoing relationship with the church, the unity or integrity of the letter, its relationship to other Pauline correspondence, and the identification and nature of the opposition. Each of these points is examined consecutively.

In terms of its history as a city, Philippi was founded around 360 BC, incorporated into the Roman province of Macedonia in 146 BC, and was the scene of a world famous military battle in 42 BC. At the time of Paul, Philippi reflected a Roman and military cast. It was strategically located, being the first station on the Egnatian Way, the gateway between Asia and the west. Religiously, the community was a potpourri of groups, brotherhoods and cult associations, dedicated to the worship of particular gods. Paul founded the church at Philippi during his second missionary journey in 48 or 49 AD in the midst of innumerable difficulties. The turbulent history of the city continued with a shameful treatment of the apostles (1 Thess 2:2), and the suffering of the community itself (1:29-30; 3:2f.; 4:2-3). However, Paul is aware of the new lease on life expressed by the Philippians, an experience he shares in terms of his own ministry in the community.

The civic group was composed primarily of pagans since there were few Jews in the area and no synagogue. Paul's converts were, therefore, Gentile Christians (3:3f.) quite unattached to Judaism. This church may be the most Gentile in composition of all the Pauline churches. Although *Acts* is not a prime source for this study, it is interesting to note that Paul's first European congregation probably consisted of women (Ac 16). In Macedonia, women were treated as the counterparts of men, and were accorded freedom and respect. Within the congregation, Evodia and Syntyche are called co-workers with Paul (4:3), and the presence of widows in the church is also suggested. Furthermore, direction, leadership and service are exercised in the community by bishops and deacons. Paul sends greetings to all the saints in the church, with their leaders (1:1). The community is diverse in its composition, yet Paul is equally fond of all the persons (1:3-8), a fact he expresses frequently.

After the founding of the Philippian church, Paul revisits Philippi and a warm supportive relationship continues to develop. Paul accepts assistance from the community (4:10-16; 2 Cor 11:9) and money for the Jerusalem collection (2 Cor 8:2-5). The church itself demonstrates further concern by sending Epaphroditus to care for the imprisoned Paul (2:25). It is surprising to witness such concern and friendship between the apostle and the community, when Paul himself acknowledges conflict and shameful treatment as a result of his initial work (1 Thess 2:2). These Christians seem to have an insight into suffering and Christian commitment

(1:29-30) that perceives different circumstances as indicators of a necessary common struggle shared by the church and its founder. Paul strongly believes that the good work begun in them will be brought to completion (1:6) since a radical transformation of life has taken place in Christ. Paul's ministry in Philippi was solid but difficult. However, during his imprisonment the very remembrance of the community seems to brighten his dismal condition (1:7) and fill him with hope (1:19). In a very solemn and personal part of the letter, Paul speaks about the possibility of his impending death (2:17). As he writes, one legal hearing was probably held with his condemnation (1:20; 2:17) or release (1:25; 2:24) imminent. However, the actual place of this incarceration of the apostle is open to discussion. The Roman origin of the letter has strong arguments and proponents. Ephesus is also a potential location for writing, but the Ephesian imprisonment of Paul cannot be documented. Caesarea, a city where Paul was in prison, is another option. The strength of the evidence seems to indicate Rome for the imprisonment with its implicit later dating of the final correspondence.[2] However, the place of origin of the letter is still an open question.

While the locale of his imprisonment cannot be determined with certainty, Paul's activity in prison is evident in the letter. An epistle is sent to the Philippians in the names of Paul and Timothy, servants of Christ Jesus (1:1). Paul obviously holds Timothy in high esteem because of his apostolic work (2:20, 22). He plans to send Timothy, who is known to the community, to Philippi so that Paul himself can receive news about the church (2:19, 23-24). Also indicated in the letter is news about Epaphroditus who was sent to Paul by the Philippians but became seriously ill before his arrival (2:25-30). The apostle is eager to send this leader and

---

[2]See Kummel, *Introduction*, p. 235, who concludes that Ephesus is the least likely place of origin; Caesarea 56-58 AD is next, Rome 58-60 is still favored until more evidence is available. Much of the discussion regarding place centers around the journeys and travels indicated in the letters. On dating, Beare, p. 24, suggests somewhere between 60-64 AD in Rome; Augrain, p. 78, is more specific, 61-62 AD.

emissary back to the group (2:28) to alleviate anxiety regarding him and Paul. In addition to this activity, Philippians also indicates the apostle's religious reflection and his exhortation to the community. These points are discussed in the following sections.

Another perspective which sheds light on the situation underlying the letter to the Philippians is the question of the integrity of the epistle. While authenticity permeates every line, the unity of the letter has been seriously questioned in the last few decades. Philippians is viewed as a composite of two, or more letters, written by Paul over a period of at least one year. In discussions on the unity of the letter, dating, an early imprisonment, future plans, new communications, community dissension and opposition are the variables analyzed.[3] A major concern for exegetes is the abrupt interruptions and brusque transitions in the letter, notably in chapter 3. However, many attribute these changes to the unusual circumstances of composition, or view them as consistent with Paul's usual vivacity and literary style. Also in favor of a unified letter is the assessment that 3:2f. be conceived as an extended postscript of specified warnings, or 3:2 - 4:3 as a long interpolation. An analysis of the content demonstrates definite motifs such as joy, contentment and confidence permeating all of the alleged sections, as well as a homogeneous set of ideas. For these reasons, Philippians is regarded as a unity in this study and as the last of Paul's letters,[4] as previously indicated.

In comparison with other Pauline epistles, Philippians is refreshing to read. The heated clashes of Galatians and Corinthians are gone, being replaced with a new understanding and acceptance (1:14-18). Likewise, Philippians is in sharp contrast to the singleminded intensity of Galatians. Paul's account of the implications of his conversion (3:4-10)

[3]See Koester, "Philippians," pp. 665-666, for a typical analysis and framework; Martin, *Philippians*, pp. 14f., for a full discussion.

[4]Beare, *Philippians*, p. 25, would regard 1:1 - 3:1; 4:2-9, 21-23 as probably the last letter, eliminating the thanksgiving letter 4:10-20. The Philippian hymn, 2:6-11, will be discussed in the interaction section.

resonates with Galatians (1:13-16) and is consistent with his customary emphasis on his vocation. While a closeness to Romans has been demonstrated, and a condensed statement on righteousness is presented (3:9), Philippians is primarily a situational rather than a theological letter. Doctrinal arguments are of little assistance in dating the letter with accuracy, whereas this perspective is important in other letters.

Finally, an understanding of the situation is enhanced by an examination of the statements and attitudes toward opposition. The Christians themselves are not intimidated by the sufferings inflicted on their apostle. In fact, they readily send gifts and continue the support of their leaders (4:15-16; 2 Cor 11:8-9). While conflict is endured by the community itself, the opponents are incapable of engendering fear among the members (1:29-30). Because the opposition is often described in general or misleading terms (1:15, 17-19; 2:21; 3:2-3), it is difficult to make a positive identification of the opponents. However, in this letter, Paul identifies the issues involved and responds to the situation of differences as an expected fact of life. He is calm and decisive (1:17; 3:2). The reality of opposition is an issue faced by Paul with his personal experience and the prison situation stimulating a balanced approach.

In the identification of the unique situation in Philippi and in an examination of Paul's relationship to the community, a foundation is laid for an understanding of the issues. While the issues in Philippians are not the fiery clashes of some of the earlier letters, they are consistent with Paul's emphasis on church life and development.

## The Issues

A cursory reading of Philippians frequently elevates a person emotionally or spiritually by offering a rare appreciation of the depth of Paul's convictions and commitment. Because of a subtle presentation and concise exposition, the problems in the community are scarcely noticed. However, upon a more careful evaluation, substantive concerns do emerge. The issues are identified as dissension within the community, diverse opposition, the imprisonment of the apostle, and the gifts of the community. Paul deals with these factions and factors in an integrated manner throughout the correspondence. However, each issue is examined separately for purposes of clarification.

Underlying many of the exhortations is an appeal for unity and likemindedness (2:1f.; 3:12f.), an emphasis that reveals a need within the community of faith. Problems of conceit and superiority (2:3), selfishness and egocentricity (2:4), and a spirit of complaining (2:14) are part of the Philippian experience. Dissension and strife are usually related to the social and communal aspects of life. The community is far from ideal in its existential experience and response (1:16-17).

In Philippians, the issue of dissension is further characterized by a very personal and pointed accusation. Evodia and Syntyche are singled out for a strong admonition by Paul (4:2). Only infrequently is such a direct insight given into church life. These women not only worked with Paul, but they also appear to have had an important role in the social world and in the community. Because of their influential status, their quarreling is harmfully affecting the church. Paul directly confronts Evodia and Syntyche, entreating them to agree. While the actual issue of disagreement is unknown, the phrase "in the Lord" suggests a religious concern. Although the apostle respects these women, he requests the community or, less likely, a mediator to intervene if necessary (4:3). Dissension within the faith community is a prime concern for Paul throughout his ministry.

The spirit of fellowship in the church is likewise adversely affected by opposition and contrary views. While Paul is not concerned about personal hostility, he certainly identifies the divisive components of the situation (1:15-18). Quite specifically, although these opponents preach Christ, they are characterized by rivalry, insincerity and unworthy motives. The missionaries seem to be taking advantage of Paul's confinement and are acting contrary to the gospel

(2:21). In fact, the partisan gospel, being presented to the community, seems to be designed to torment Paul.

A further threat affects the Philippian church. Paul identifies another group of opponents as "dogs," evil-workers and mutilators of the flesh (3:2). While "dogs" is a term customarily used for the Gentiles, Paul may here be hurling this insulting expression of derision and disdain at his own people. Whether these intruders are Jewish Christians, Hellenistic Jews or gnostics is difficult to ascertain. However, they do advocate circumcision and present a real and dangerous threat to the community (3:18-19). Called enemies of the cross of Christ by Paul (3:18), they set themselves up as models of Christian leadership. Vice is made into virtue (3:19 and a contradictory and destructive example is being given by them to the community.

The opposition brings some deeper problems to the surface. For example, although the opponents share Paul's conviction that the ultimate goal is Christ Jesus (3:7-16), they seem also to preach a radical spiritualistic eschatology. This misguided eschatology not only fails to grasp the significance of the cross, but also distorts the view of Christian life by offering perfection rather than a paschal perspective. There is evidence in the letter that a loss of eschatological hope will eventually distort the Philippian understanding of the gospel itself (1:6, 10, 28; 2:16; 4:5). The appeal and the strength of the opposition constitutes an issue that must be addressed.

The imprisonment of the apostle and the threat of death embody a very personal issue for Paul with important consequences for the community. For a person of Paul's temperament, shackles must have been a very trying experience. As he reflects on his situation, Paul seems to oscillate between the expectation of death and a continuation of his earthly life (1:19-26; 2:17, 24; 3:12-14). Even though he refers to his imprisonment several times (1:13, 14, 17; 2:12, 17), he consistently speaks of its effects on the preaching of the gospel (1:12-13). Because he is a Christian, and because of his work for Christ, Paul is being detained. However, Christ is still made known by his imprisonment and Paul's

mission is ironically advanced by the boldness of his followers (1:14). The Philippians must admire the perspective and
the tone of the founder of their church, as he directs his
attention to them (1:3f.) and reflects on the true meaning of
life (1:20-21). While the imprisonment is an issue for Paul
and for the church, it does not appear to be an insurmounta-
ble obstacle. Rather, it is an unfortunate situation to be
accepted and utilized. Paul sees this suffering as a point of
contact and union with the Christ Paul proclaims (3:10).
Therefore, the issue is a stepping stone to the ultimate
success of his Christian life and ministry.

Finally, in what some commentators have identified as a
letter of thanks (4:10-20), Paul acknowledges the concern of
the community for him. Their gifts have been generous and
consistent and bring joy to the apostle (4:10-11). Epaphroditus, the bearer of a recent gift (4:18), will soon return to
Philippi (2:25 29). The Philippians have been supportive in
sending the person Epaphroditus as well as in their monetary assistance. Although Paul never uses actual expressions of thanks in this section, his feelings are evident. In
speaking of a detachment while still acknowledging his
dependence on them (4:10-11), Paul skillfully deals with a
kind of support he was reluctant to accept in Corinth. The
issue of gifts has a personal flavor although it represents a
mutual acceptance of apostle and community.

The considerations in Philippians are neither unexpected
nor intricate. However, they do epitomize some of the unique aspects of Paul's relationship to this church and a very
unique period in his life.


## Interaction and Response


Paul's imprisonment affords him the opportunity of
interacting with the Philippian community under very unusual circumstances. The letter reveals a very personal relationship between Paul and the community, addresses the
issue of dissension, presents a perspective on Christian life,
and reveals an insight into the spirituality of Paul. The

apostle deals with opposition and plans a strategy for the continued development of the Philippian church. In this warm and moving letter, the leader is observed, possibly in his final days. His thoughts, priorities and perspectives are presented for the congregation to witness and to contemplate.

In the Philippian correspondence, Paul's relationship to the community is consistently warm, deep, affectionate and filled with gratitude. Paul and the community not only liked each other, but the apostle is filled with love in his very remembrance of them (1:3-8). Paul is profuse in his affirmation and in his appreciation of the church. They are his friends and partners in the gospel (1:5, 7), his joy and crown (4:1). He yearns deeply for an opportunity to be personally present, while assuring them of his continued affection (1:8). Not only did this church cause him very few problems, but they openly supported him in his missionary endeavors when he had cause for discouragement (4:15-16). The apostle acknowledges their generosity and support, using Philippi as an example for others (2 Cor 8:1-5).

Within the usual thanksgiving of the letter (1:3f.), Paul reveals his deep feeling for the church. This unique relationship contributes to the setting of a joyful tone and also underlies the radiant character of the letter's prayer passages. The thanksgiving arises out of and is intimately connected to the situation of the apostle and the congregation. Furthermore, in his acknowledgement of their gift, Paul delicately expresses his appreciation (4:10f.), while reiterating Christian values of indifference to wealth or poverty. Again, Paul demonstrates his ability to give and to win affection by his attitude and approval (4:18-20). In his final greetings (4:21-22), the apostle acknowledges the individual members of the community, a further example of the quality of his relationship with the members of this church. If Philippians is the most personal of Paul's letters, and his relationship with the community the most affectionate, this reality does not inhibit the apostle in his ability to confront issues.

After confirming his motivation (4:1), Paul deals openly

with Evodia and Syntyche in their disagreement. The attitude of openness is evident elsewhere in the letter as Paul takes the time to explain his situation to his friends (1:1-2). With these women, there is an acknowledgement of the difficulty, a personal entreaty to them, and an alternative if they cannot sort out the problem themselves (4:2-3). Nowhere does Paul attempt to suppress these persons or diminish their influence within the community. However, the restoration of good order and peace is insured by Paul in his approach.

The apostle likewise addresses this issue of dissension and disunity by his admonitions to the community. As he encourages the Philippians toward unity (2:2) and explicitly identifies appropriate Christian attitudes (2:3-5; 4:8), Evodia and Syntyche and all the members of the congregation must pause and examine themselves. While Paul is able to confront persons when necessary, he also indirectly strengthens his purpose by general comments and criticisms.

Within the exhortations and the letter itself, there is a dynamic presentation of Christian life. Paul focuses on joy, hope and the centrality of the cross in order to present an ideal and, thereby, address the problems in the community. While it is relatively easy to determine the appeal of the cross to an apostle in prison, it is more difficult to understand the perspective of joy as an integral part of life. Yet, joy and fellowship are identified as the dominating themes in Philippians.

Paul frequently cautions against divisiveness (1:27-28); more importantly, he presents the life of the Christian as a participation in the life of Christ. Briefly, though effectively in this letter, he identifies the new righteousness and Christ's resurrection as the direction and force in Christian life (3:9-11). Union with and transformation in Christ is the reason for joy and hope during times of intense suffering. Furthermore, Paul views all present experiences in terms of the final end (2:1; 4:8). The careful balance and creative tension which result, offer objectivity on the level of faith and pave the way for a radical response to the distress of the existential situation. Because of these perspectives, Paul can encourage the community to a consistently difficult religious witness. It is within this context that Christian joy must be understood.

The theme of joy permeates the letter to the Philippians (1:18, 25; 2:2, 17, 18, 28, 29; 3:1; 4:1, 4, 10). Not only does Paul radiate serenity and contentment (1:3-12), but the church itself is encouraged along these lines (3:1). The apostle, however, does not rely on natural optimism or the feelings of the moment. Rather, he appeals to the faith of the community in order to insure a truly Christian response under stress (4:4). Although Paul could gain great sympathy because of his situation, he chooses to utilize the moment for the qualitative building up of the church.

Likewise, hope, a virtue which for the Christian presumes faith, is encouraged by Paul. Assurances built on experience, are offered to the community; the good work begun in them will be brought to completion (1:6). The new life of the Christian is the work of God and not a product of human achievement. This perspective underlies the exhortations of Paul (3:16; 4:5; 3:20-21), and enables him to exercise leadership with an eye toward the future. Peace is promised (4:7) and anxiety is inauthentic (4:6), even though the struggle for salvation will continue (2:12-18).

Although he offers hope and radiates joy, Paul is keenly aware of the dynamics and the rhythms of Christian existence. While there is a goal and a prize (3:14), the race must be run (3:12-13). Through these vivid cultural images of the athletic games, Paul expresses his conviction that commitment is an ongoing process and struggle.

Finally, the paschal experience of Christian life is presented as Paul incorporates an early Christian hymn into his exhortations (2:6-11).[5] While the hymn has been studied from a variety of perspectives, offering diverse interpreta-

---

[5]For the origin of the hymn, see Kummel, *Introduction*, p. 237; Stanley, *Christ's Resurrection*, p. 102; Beare, *Philippians*, p. 1; Koester, "Philippians," p. 666; Murphy-O'Connor, "Philippians 2:6-11," p. 26; Howard, "Philippians 2: 6-11," p. 386; Mann, "Philippians 2:6-11," p. 10; Eckmann, "Hymn," p. 258.

tions, Paul uses the unit to present Christ as the model for the community (2:5). The Philippians are urged to conform to the pattern of Christ, a pattern of obedience, of humility, of death and exaltation. More than a hymn to the divinity of Christ, it is a challenge for those who are in Christ to nurture appropriate dispositions. Humility and abasement are the necessary attitudes for the Philippian church. While a christology is presented in this passage, the consequences for humanity and the asceticism of the cross (2:8),[6] are the primary concerns of Paul. The controlling factor in Pauline ethics is the paschal cycle of dying and rising with Christ. As the apostle exhorts the community to a deeper Christian life, he reminds them of Christ, who emptied Himself (2:7) and was subsequently exalted by God (2:8). This pattern, lived out in faith, constitutes the essence of Christian life, a pattern which Paul himself is experiencing.

The often friendly conversation of Philippians assumes another dimension as Paul gives moving testimony to the depth of his own spirituality in chapter 3. It is a spirituality dominated by a deep commitment to Christ and an apostolic orientation. The centrality of Christ is a constant (3:8, 10, 12, 14), directing every aspect of Paul's life. The apostle shares with the Philippians a harsh assessment of his cultural and religious background (3:4-6). Not only is everything counted as worthless (3:7-8), but Paul actually parts company with Judaism because of his knowledge of Christ. This willingness to reject what has been cherished, because of his Christian commitment, is a challenge to the church. Paul now presses on toward the attainment of his goal, devoting himself to this pursuit totally and with unremitting energy (3:12-13).

However, Paul does not simply reflect personal goals. As he reveals some of his innermost thoughts, he quickly turns

----

[6]The concept of kenosis has been discussed frequently. See *IDB* Vol. 3, p. 7, for a developmental understanding. The article notes that the term "kenosis" was first used in the 3rd and 4th centuries to express the idea in Philippians 2:7; Finley, "Kenosis," relates the attitude to Christian life; Greehy, pp. 1195-1196, discusses kenosis and the kenotic ideal for the Christian; Caird, *Prison*, p. 121, states there is no justification for a kenotic christology.

to apostolic interests and endeavors (3:15f.). This apostolic orientation is characteristic of the entire correspondence and is indicative of the thrust of Paul's lived spirituality. He appreciates loyalty and solace during the evening of his life, but his personal concerns are consistently overshadowed by the needs of the church. Giving attention to others through time and ministry in a spirit of sincerity and honesty is the approach the apostle assumes. Ironically, his imprisonment is advancing the gospel and offering witness to a broad audience (1:12-13). Therefore, Paul exudes a confidence (1:18, 26-27) and a spirit of rejoicing (1:19) as he relies on the continued prayers of the church.

While Paul expresses an ambivalence toward life or death in this letter (1:21-23), his spirituality is such that he is motivated by union with Christ in both instances. His attitude is not an escape from life but rather a faithful following of the Lord. Furthermore, Paul explicitly mentions his apostolic concerns within this context, demonstrating again that his ministry assumes precedence over his own personal desires (1:24). The dual prongs of the spirituality of Paul, a commitment to Christ and to ministry, is exemplified in this powerful letter. While apostolic spirituality is a contemporary expression, it rightly describes the apostle to the Gentiles in his lived Christian experience.

Paul's interaction with the Philippian church is motivated by religious commitment, permeated with Christian values and conditioned by his own imprisonment. In his treatment of opposition these forces converge. While Paul identifies the opponents in harsh and degrading terms (3:2; 2:21), indicating judgment and understanding, he seems to give up debating with his adversaries. He appears more willing to take opposition in stride as long as the gospel is proclaimed and Christian purposes advanced (1:18). Maturity enters into this perspective as Paul assumes the Philippians' ability to discern and to know the true revelation of God (3:15). Paul may be sensitive to opposition (1:17; 3:18) but he is not intimidated by it (1:28-29). The ability to distance himself enables Paul to present a dynamic view of Christian life that addresses the underlying issues of the opposition. He also portrays righteousness in a new perspective as well as offering a reassessment of his own Jewish heritage (3:3f.). Points are made, but undue attention is not given to differing perspectives within or outside of the community. Rather, the Philippians are prepared for meeting diversity and evaluating it by the apostle and his teaching (3:16-17). Finally, insight into Paul's strategy for the future is evident in Philippians. In regard to local leaders and colleagues, Paul acknowledges the presence of influential persons in the community (1:1; 4:2) and solicits their assistance in resolving difficulties (4:3). He also plans to send Timothy, a respected co-worker, to the community to insure the continuation of his apostolic endeavors (2:19-24). Paul is probably hesitant about the possibility of his own release from prison, and therefore, sends a person of stature in his stead. The choice is an excellent one since Timothy not only understands Paul because of their close association, but also he is no stranger to the church. The apostle likewise recognizes and utilizes Epaphroditus (2:25-30), an esteemed local leader. In sending him back to the community, Paul's purpose is to relieve a personal and group anxiety. The emotional tone of the group is an important consideration for the apostle.

A deep sense of responsibility for the church is demonstrated in Paul's concrete actions on behalf of the church. Furthermore, he anticipates the difficulties of the group when he is no longer alive. Imitation of all who witness to Christ's presence is advocated (3:17), and a remembrance of Paul's teaching is encouraged (4:9). Continual obedience and commitment to Christian values (2:12), is strongly urged in Paul's absence, for he certainly does not want to have labored in vain in Philippi (2:16). The ultimate goal of salvation is to be shared by Paul and their church. Paul attempts to insure this outcome by his responsiveness to the issues and concerns within the community. However, the entire letter is conditioned by Paul's own imprisonment and his assessment of it. "Christ will be honored, in my body, whether by my life or by my death. For to me to live is Christ, and to die is gain" (1:20-21).

## Assessment of Leadership

In his last public letter, considerable insight is gained into a formidable and effective early Christian leader. Paul's personal and pastoral character, as well as his extraordinary commitment, are clearly presented in his response to the Christian congregation in Philippi. To facilitate the assessment of Paul's leadership in this correspondence, the following perspectives are examined: the quality of his religious leadership, his response to the situation, his ability to change his leadership style and the degree of acceptance of and by the community.

The leadership exercised by Paul in Philippians is correctly described as *religious leadership*. Paul's responses and assessments are motivated by strong religious convictions and goals (1:19f.). There are no secondary distractions in this letter. Rather, the life of Christ and life in Christ determine conditions and affect the exhortations and theological reflections. Philippians is an important witness to Pauline spirituality (3:2f.) in conveying Paul's total identification with Christ and with the mission of Christ. Not only is Paul dedicated to religious integration and spiritual progress (3:12), but Christian life itself is presented as a continual discovery of what it means to be grasped by Christ.

The apostle describes himself as a servant (1:1), just as Christ himself assumed this identity (2:7). As an active spiritual leader, Paul challenges the Philippian church to cultivate this same mind and orientation in themselves (2:5). He also offers them models to emulate in himself and others (3:17). Furthermore, while Paul utilizes all the human resources available to him and his own personal qualities to clarify and to argue his position, his ultimate enlightenment is from the Lord (3:15). The apostle's understanding of the gospel and of ministry is permeated and enlivened by his prayer and intercessions. During a difficult imprisonment, Paul consistently expresses his total reliance on Christ and interprets the final outcome of Christian life according to this standard. In facing death, Paul ponders the deepest realities of his existence. He also shares his longings, priorities and inner strength with the community (1:21).

As a religious leader, Paul places the interests and needs of the church above his own desires. In this respect, he incarnates the ideal of a servant style of leadership.

Another component in Paul's leadership in Philippians is his responsiveness to a unique situation. Although a *situational approach* is characteristic of Paul's efforts in other communities, the fact of his imprisonment incorporates a new dimension. Paul exercises his authority as apostle and founder of the church at Philippi by affirming (1:3-8), encouraging (2:1-2), exhorting (1:27f.; 2:3-4) and confronting (4:2) the community. The issues in this letter reveal that even this very special community is part of a human church, struggling toward a final goal (3:14). Because of a consideration of his experience and his options, Paul seems to mellow in his dealings with opposition (1:18). Consequently, he focuses on the community as a priority and portrays communal life and attitudes in terms of unity, service and joy (2:5; 4:4).

Although there are theological reflections in the letter to the Philippians, a pastoral and situational response is the prime concern of Paul. The occasion of quarreling (4:2) is a good example of a leader's requirement to confront a delicate situation because of gospel values. Furthermore, Paul, hampered by his internment, seeks alternatives to reinstate these women and diminish any negative vibrations within the group (4:3).

Furthermore, because of his own constraints, Paul delegates responsibility (2:19f.) and prepares the group for his sustained absence (2:12). A spirit of detachment is appropriately expressed by Paul with regard to many circumstances of life (1:23; 4:12). This ability to distance himself seems to enable Paul not only to accept his fate, but also to offer more realistic solutions to problems. There is no defensiveness in Philippians, but rather a steady reflection on the overriding goals of the gospel (1:18). With these values uppermost in his mind, Paul exercises a confident and a controlled leadership.

The spirit and tone of Philippians reveals an *ability to*

*change* on the part of Paul. No longer is combat constitutive of his style, but rather a confident and hopeful approach. Paul has a sustained capacity to look beyond immediate irritations and disturbances to future outcomes and goals. His sobering experience in Corinth seems to have been effective in augmenting this change. Furthermore, Paul is now more prone to delegate responsibility to others who are acceptable to the congregation. Leaders are recognized, acknowledged and utilized by Paul in addition to his customary facilitating of communal responsibility (1:1; 2:19f.; 4:3). Again, the apostle's movement along these lines is dictated by his Christian commitment. Furthermore, Paul seems to simplify issues in this letter; there is little elaboration on the implications of opposition and diversity. With brevity, he presents his theological reflections and his spiritual insights (3:2f.). As Paul moves toward the termination of his life and active ministry, he rejects the restraints of his Jewish past and surges forward to a complete transformation of his life in Christ.

Finally, an unusual degree of *mutual acceptance* underlines the entire correspondence. When a reciprocal high regard is operative in a relationship, a new freedom is experienced by the leader and the group. Persons grow and develop when empathy, understanding, acceptance, and trust form the relational bonds.[7] Furthermore, the excellent relationship between Paul and the community enables him strongly to suggest options (1:19-26; 3:3-17), and to act appropriately (2:19f.; 4:2f.). Affirmation and love does not paralyze the apostle into ineffective behavior. Rather, these qualities enable Paul and the community to deal with the harsh realities of existence (1:12f.; 3:1f). Paul's authentic personal relationship with the church allows him to accept financial and human support, and also facilitates the depth

---

[7]Greenleaf, *Servant Leadership*, p. 21, states it well: "People grow taller when those who lead them empathize and when they are accepted for what they are, even though their performance may be judged critically in terms of what they are capable of doing. Leaders who empathize and who fully accept those who go with them on this basis are more likely to be trusted."

of intimate sharing that constitutes the Philippian letter. This reality of personal interaction and service is a strong challenge to the "professional" religious leader of today. In the letter to Paul's first European congregation, written toward the culmination of his ministry, a personal and apostolic maturity is crystalized. The apostle is able to encounter the threat of death with equanimity and detachment. Likewise, he approaches his apostolic endeavors with similar attitudes. Because of the personal human support and a realistically tested spirituality, Paul emerges as a religious leader par excellence. The caliber and quality of his leadership emerges as he begins to relinquish his position, while ensuring the future growth of the church. His attitudes and efforts deserve admiration and emulation.

# CONCLUSION

# PAUL THE LEADER

In the examination of the letters of Paul from the perspective of his leadership in the early church, the variety of Paul's responses to persons and to issues is clearly identified. The apostle appears to be a leader who assesses situations and then acts accordingly. In the dynamic interaction and response so evident in the letters, Paul not only encourages and challenges contemporary Christian leaders, but he often models the essential qualities of religious leadership itself. Therefore, a focus on Paul's leadership and the implications for today is appropriate.

## *The Evidence*

The leadership of Paul is graphically portrayed in the New Testament letters authentically his, namely, 1 Thessalonians, Galatians, 1 and 2 Corinthians, Romans, and Philippians. These letters reflect the times as well as the person, the concerns as well as the potential solutions. While the early church was certainly in the midst of a crisis in terms of its relationship to Judaism, the Pauline letters offer the contemporary reader more than first century background and information. Because of the nature of the Christian tradition, scriptural insights can significantly affect the present situation. The crisis of leadership in the church today can be addressed from this biblical perspective.

In the correspondence of the apostle Paul, the thoughts, expressions and interaction of a single personality emerge. The letters are potentially a key to the development and the changes in the style of an early church leader. However, this leader operates from a certain religious perspective and consciousness. In this regard, Paul's exercise of leadership and the source of his strength challenge committed Christians in every age.

With *1 Thessalonians*, Paul initially and creatively utilizes letter writing as a substitute for his apostolic presence. As an apostle, he operates from a convinced and committed Christian vision of life, establishing his authority from God Himself. Paul is aware of the situation and concerns of the community, has a good relationship with his converts and is willing to utilize co-workers by delegation. Communal life and responsibility are an important focus. Paul's success is attributed to his confidence, a personal relationship with the community and a realistic, situational approach. In this earliest letter, excellent leadership potential is evident.

The letter to the *Galatians* represents an initial questioning of the Pauline gospel and the emergence of a major issue, the identity and relationship between Jew and Gentile. Paul not only identifies the underlying issue but prioritizes his concerns and presents the christological implications of various approaches. As a leader, Paul defends, confronts, attacks, presents and argues. He forces the community to assess the implications of issues at stake by use of his gifts of persuasion, his literary and rhetorical skills. The situation is addressed directly as Paul establishes his apostolic authority. In dealing with conflict and controversy, confrontation and anger are his initial response. However, both a positive and negative assessment of his leadership can be substantiated.

In the diverse *Corinthian* correspondence, specific issues, a changing situation, consecutive letters and visits, are identified. This community has a penchant for misunderstanding Paul, and in 1 Corinthians Paul responds to questions and reports existentially and theologically. In 2 Corinthians, opposition to Paul is evident and he reacts by carefully establishing his apostolic authority and boasting of his credentials. In the earlier letter Paul creatively deals with diversity, opposing some views while establishing a strategy for the identification and application of principles. He uses persuasion, modeling, argument, and judgment in order to elicit a positive response. However, when Paul is under attack, and subject to the extremes of controversy and diversity, he reacts. In an all too personal response in 2 Corinthians, the apostle is defensive in his approach to the issue. However, a certain stamina and resiliency are apparent as Paul reassesses his ministry.

The theologian emerges full force in the letter to the *Romans*. Although Paul never visited the community, he identifies the central problem as the Jewish/Gentile relationship with some secondary components. A new integration and maturing is apparent as Paul raises the church's theological consciousness and clarifies issues and implications. Paul urges communal responsibility and facilitates their judgment in difficult situations by using broad and global examples and perspectives. Through this letter, Paul prepares himself and the congregation for future encounters and interaction.

The imprisonment of Paul during the writing of *Philippians* offers another kind of distance and another perspective. A joy, contentment and confidence radiate through the passages. The futurist perspective is the measuring rod for Paul's life and ministry. A distinctly Christian perspective is poignantly presented as Paul reveals his apostolic spirituality. As a religious leader, the apostle prepares the community for his absense, recognizes leadership in the community, and delegates responsibility to colleagues. An unusual degree of mutual love and acceptance enables the leader to relinquish his unique position in order to ensure the growth of the church.

## The Leader

Any assessment of Paul as a leader must take into account several prime factors. As a person, Paul encompasses greatness and limitations, gifts and liabilities. His personal qualities are strong and dynamic making him undoubtedly the focal point in the early Christian churches. Vision and commitment are always evident and exemplary in his words and responses. Indeed, Paul is a religious leader who identifies his unique call and conversion as the turning point in his life. He understands his apostolic mission in terms of this experience and preaches the gospel because of the Lord's revelation to him. Furthermore, Paul's authority is established consistently as from the Lord, an authority to be exercised as a servant of others. Finally, Paul responds to the unique situation and the issues in the various churches. He is able to deal with diversity with varying degrees of success and with a spectrum of leadership styles. A versatility and resiliency characterize the person who interacts in the letters. However, the presence of the Spirit of the Lord directs and dominates Paul's perspective on Christian life and ministry. Guided by religious goals and principles, the situations and issues are perceived as vehicles for growth. Therefore, any assessment of Paul as a leader must take into account his personal attributes, his religious convictions, his exercise of a unique authority and his unique situational responses.

On an evaluative level, this study reveals again the positive and negative dimensions of Paul's leadership. A Christian vision of life and of ultimate goals directs Paul's approach to the communities identified in the letters. His mission and ministry likewise emanate from a profound religious experience. However, while Paul is committed to his apostolic calling and endeavors, he is sometimes too attached to his success and loses perspective in his response, as indicated in 2 Corinthians.

Paul has an ability to work with a variety of groups. In Thessalonica and Philippi, a good personal relationship and a deep empathy enable him to affirm the community, challenge them on the level of growth and accept suffering because of his theological convictions and beliefs. In Galatia and Corinth, conflict, opposition and controversy enable Paul to identify issues and to present clear and strong theological foundations for his positions. At times he becomes too personally involved, but more consistently, crisis and opposition facilitate a confronting and elucidating leadership style. With the Roman community, Paul likewise, clarifies, presents and addresses issues in substantial and theologically creative ways, even though he has no first hand acquaintance with the congregation.

As a leader Paul facilitates the growth of the group while maintaining his strong influence and persuasive appeal. He encourages participation but also uses directive forms of leadership. In delegating he maintains his leverage and input on the central issues. Paul tends to delegate and to share more freely when a good mutual relationship exists. He is hesitant with the problem churches.

Not only does Paul exercise his leadership in a variety of churches, but he also relates to a broad spectrum of persons. With select colleagues, he shares deeply, developing and honing their leadership skills. He seeks to serve rather than to dominate, placing a high priority on personal affirmation and support.

Paul exercises theological leadership in all his letters but notably in Romans, Galatians and 1 Corinthians. The unique leadership response shown in the letters is developed in a dynamic fashion as Paul is challenged by different situations, groups and issues. On the other hand, he also believes in the ability of the community to discern the truth in faith.

Finally, Paul relies on a variety of resources, background, traditions, gifts, colleagues, and the Lord Himself to spread the gospel message. He is a creative, dynamic and enterprising leader who is ultimately forgiven his mistakes because of his sincerity and profound religious convictions.

A leadership person who utilizes a variety of approaches is clearly identified in the correspondence. Paul is a powerful example as a religious leader, and offers a perspective on leadership that withstands the test of time. There are key insights into the appropriate exercise of leadership for the committed Christian who must deal continually with crisis, challenge, development and change.

## Implications and Reflections

Although there is no best leadership style and no best strategy for change, the most effective leaders adapt and augment their responses according to environmental and situational demands. Likewise, there is no ideal leader or leadership approach. Rather, leadership is an interactional response between leaders and followers in various and unique situations. While this assessment is certainly true for Paul, his religious convictions consistently determine the parameters and the quality of his response. He has experienced the Lord, and he has a Christian vision of life. In the contemporary church, the exercise of Christian leadership should integrate acceptable and effective leadership approaches with religious values. Leadership styles must be consistent with a personal and corporate religious identity. Paul is a model and an exemplar in the sphere of religious leadership.

As an apostle, Paul exercises his leadership during a period of crisis in the early church. Not only is there opposition within the communities, but there is as well the gradual separation of Christians from their Jewish roots. Critical issues emerge, and a radical reorientation affects persons, families and groups. New, fresh, theological reflection results as the difficulties are addressed by Paul. In the contemporary situation, the church is in another critical stage in its identity and growth. Roles, ministries, essence, identity are all being questioned. If the letters of Paul offer any insight, it is that crisis can lead to growth. However, Christian leadership and theological vision are key factors in facilitating the appropriate responses within the community of faith.

Paul's leadership was significantly affected by the followers he encountered. The dynamics between these two entities can be dramatic and forceful. Responsibilities are heavy on the part of both groups. In the contemporary church, persons in leadership positions are subject to an extraordinary amount of criticism and confrontation. While Paul offers insights into dealing with opposition, it must be noted that the most personally satisfying experiences and the deepest spiritual insights are evident in the communities in which mutual esteem, respect, support and affirmation exist. Today, leaders and followers are challenged to create this type of atmosphere so all persons can offer their real gifts to the church.

Finally, Paul's leadership effectiveness is not necessarily positively correlated with the amount of time he spends with individuals or with the communities. Corinth was his place of residence for a long period of time and the recipient of four letters from the founder of the church. Yet, the theological depth of Romans is not achieved in these letters, nor the revealing spirituality permeating the letter to the Philippians. Perhaps leisure and distance are essential ingredients if a maturity and refinement in leadership and vision are to be achieved. The "burned out" leaders of the church would do well to pause, to assess and integrate experience and theology. With an integrated leadership approach, a qualitatively different level of interaction and life will begin to emerge in the church.

Paul is a religious leader of unique caliber and quality. He is prophetic and charismatic, a servant and an apostle. For him, to live is Christ, and so the proclamation of the gospel and the building of the church summon all his energy and commitment. Early in Paul's ministry, he exhorts a community in the sensitive and critical area of its responsibility toward its leaders. As Paul subsequently encounters a wide range of responses during his missionary activity, he must have poignantly recalled those words. If lived out in a Christian sense, the words and the attitudes they encourage would foster the continued growth and development not only of leaders, but of the entire church. How important it is that the church listen to Paul today. "But we beseech you, brethren, to respect those who labor among you and are over you in the Lord and admonish you, and to esteem them very highly in love because of their work" (1 Th 5:12-13a).

# *APPENDIX*

# GLOSSARY

The descriptive definitions of the following significant terms may be helpful to the reader in understanding the biblical and/or the twentieth century concepts of authority, power and leadership.

The writer relies on authors cited in the text for these composite definitions, notably Stanley, McKenzie, Holmberg and Schutz for *authority* and related concepts; Schutz, Hersey and Blanchard, Burns and Greenleaf for *power* and *leadership*. The categories and basic synthesis of types of power in Hersey and Blanchard, pp. 178-179 is particularly helpful and is utilized in this glossary.

## *Authority*

*Authority*: The understanding of authority within the church is created by Jesus himself and has its source in the dynamic presence of the exalted Christ. This authority explains, persuades and points the way toward the future. It is more of a creative power as opposed to an external force; the term "exousia" designates authority as a Christian reality. All Christians participate in Christ's authority in varying degrees and the cultural expressions of authority are continually adapted to changing needs. In the letters, Paul is already an authority figure but his claims rest on *an apostolic authority* manifested in his preaching of the good news. Authority in the Pauline churches is shared, and is one of the many functions of the one Spirit in the one body.

Christian authority is likewise an expression of *diakonia* or service. Authority implies social relationships within the community that is church and a developmental understanding. New Testament authority commends itself by persuading and convincing, by a personal leadership approach, by a participatory stance, and by an active and authentic love.

*Charismatic authority*: This authority implies the utilization of the gifts of the Spirit for Paul and the individual members of the churches. It is a highly personal, and legitimate form of authority.

*Legitimacy:* Not only is legitimacy related to authority, but it is also an interpretation of authority. Legitimacy answers the question of why one exercises authority. For Paul, it is based on his call and the gospel of God, a divine legitimacy.

*Office:* There is no equivalent term in the New Testament; rather *ministry* is utilized as a function or gift of the Spirit.

*Admonitions:* These are perceived as challenges or urgings which respect the spiritual freedom and independence of the churches. They bear little resemblance to orders or imperatives. Implied in the use of admonitions is a sense of commitment which elicits a response because of internal sanctions or motivations.

*Co-workers:* This group includes the collaborators who travelled and worked with Paul. Many such as Mark, Titus, Aquila and Prisca have a long-term relationship with Paul. Others such as Timothy, Titus and Mark are subordinate to him. Silvanus seems to be an equal.

*Presbyteros-episcopos:* These persons were usually leaders and teachers in the community.

## Power

*Power:* Authority and power are often intertwined. Power is perceived as the source of authority, and authority is another side of power as it interprets it and makes it accessible. Paul's sense of power is dominated by the cross, a power in weakness and weakness as power. The apostle also resonates with the Old Testament view of the Spirit as an animating power or force. This view is interwoven into his view of church which sees the power of the Spirit at work in all the members and which is manifested in different works. In fact, Spirit and power are almost synonymous. Power has influence potential which in turn leads to compliance. This power results from position or the person himself. In Paul, both are seen as being persuasive because of his position as an apostle and his personal relationship with the community.

*Coercive power* is based on fear. In the use of this power a leader induces compliance because failure will lead to punishment.

*Legitimate power* is based on the position held by the leader. A leader in a high position can use legitimate power to induce compliance or influence others. The leader is perceived as having the right, by virtue of his/her position in the organization or group, to expect that suggestions will be followed.

*Expert power* is based on the leader's possession of expertise, skill and knowledge, which is utilized to influence others. This leader is seen as possessing the expertise to facilitate the work behavior of others. Respect on the part of others leads to compliance.

*Connection power* results from the leader's "connections" with important persons inside or outside the organization. Compliance from others is achieved because persons are concerned about the favor or the disfavor of the powerful connection.

*Information power* results from the leader's possession of or access to information considered valuable by others. People are influenced because they need or want this information.

*Referent power* is based on the leader's personal traits. This leader is generally liked and admired by others because of personality. Others are influenced by their admiration for and identification with the leader.

*Reward power* is identified when the leader has the ability to provide rewards or bonuses for others. It is incentive oriented.

# Leadership

*Leadership*: is the ability to affect others' actions or attitudes in a dynamic manner. It involves an interplay between leaders and followers and is usually directed toward an end or purpose.

*Situational Leadership:* This form of leadership uses a variety of styles in direct response to unique circumstances and to the level of maturity in the group. The ability to diagnose the situation is essential as well as the conviction that followers should be helped in their growth toward maturity. Maturity is understood as the person's ability and willingness to take responsibility for the direction of their own lives and behavior. This approach to leadership also implies the ability to change and to be flexible because of group itself, culture and social situations. Responsibility is a requirement for leaders and followers in terms of sharing their perceptions of social reality. Implied are varying degrees of relational bonds, appropriate to the existential purposes and situations.

*Charismatic leadership:* This style of leadership is based on the utilization of the gifts of the Spirit as an expression of authority in the early New Testament period, and as directed to a particular goal. The leader can be considered charismatic but also implied is the facilitating of the gifts of others in the community in response to the unique situational needs.

*Prophetic leadership:* This form of leadership challenges, confronts and encourages the community in terms of religious convictions and ultimate goals. For Paul, personal relationships often define the community situation as well as his Christian call, contributing to his unique use of this style beyond that of the Hebrew prophets.

*Servant leadership:* Servant leadership is acting upon belief. In the early church *diakonia* constitutes the unique Christian approach to authority and ministry. It is a leadership style fostered at all levels within the Christian community, thereby encouraging participation.

*Moral leadership:* This leadership style can also be described as *transforming leadership.* In the letters of Paul, it is the result of being in Christ and focuses on the implications for Christian life.

# ANNOTATED BIBLIOGRAPHY ON RELIGIOUS LEADERSHIP

Although the reader of this book is very familiar with the usual biblical resources, the topic of leadership may be an emerging interest. The following annotated bibliography on religious leadership, while not exhaustive, represents some of the more accessible materials on the subject.

Ashton, J. "Authority in the Gospel." *Way* (1972), p.211-221.

This fine article examines the New Testament concept of authority. For Christ, authority is an authority of truth, derived from the Father. The Christian's authority is like that of Christ and it must be seen primarily in terms of service not power.

Basil, Douglas C. "Leadership Skills and the Crisis of Change." *Humanitas*, 14 (1978), pp. 309-320.

The dimensions of change are examined by the author. Technological change affects and demands social, behavioral and structural, institutional changes. A leader must assess the environment, be a strategist, motivator, decision-maker, and implementor. The paradigm of leadership skills demanded by the crisis of change in society is increasingly responsive skills as opposed to traditional or transitional ones utilized up to the 1970's. The ability to deal with ambiquity, conflict, and complexity is also essential. The principles in this article can speak to church leadership questions.

Beeson, Trevor. "Leadership's Exhausting and Hazardous Besides." *The Christian Century: A Ecumenical Weekly.*, 98(1981), pp. 790-791.

Brief reflections on several leaders, John Paul II, Barbara Ward, Robert Runcie, are written in news briefing style.

Beloin, Robert L. "Leadership: A Matter of Quality." *Studies in Formative Spirituality*, 3(1982), pp. 13-24.

The author sees leadership in the spiritual life as demanding a deep immersion into that life by the leader. Roots in a biblical spirituality, and awareness of the traditions of the early church are essential. A dynamic and solid definition of Christian spirituality is presented and the possession of certain gifts which will inspire and challenge persons on their faith journey are considered essential. The gifts are prophetic insight, attentive listening and poverty for service. The article is a fine overview of the topic.

Boos, Virginia, Sister, OSF. "Spirituality and Prophetic Leadership in Catholic Education." *Sisters Today* 53 (1981), pp. 25-31.

Catholic educators are viewed as leaders and prophets by the author. A religious climate and prayer are essential for receiving the prophetic call. In the Hebrew Bible, prophets challenge, heal, reconcile, and witness. Contemporary prophecy is further characterized by personal rerooting, creativity, community orientation, reluctance or hesitancy, and creative suffering. The call implies mission. The article offers an overview to an understanding of prophetic leadership but leaves most of the application to the reader.

Brinkman, Marie, Sister, SCL. "Religious Leadership and the Ministry of Justice." *Sisters Today*, 52(1980), pp. 588-595.

The article focuses on a leader, profoundly inspired by justice and by her relationship to her religious community. A discerning spirit is able to identify the talent of each person in a community. A discernment of the voice of the Spirit is essential in individuals and in groups. Compassion and justice illuminating the vows and their power in a communal way of life are discussed. The principles can be applied to broader leadership in the church.

Byron, William. J., SJ. "The Purpose and Nature of Leadership." *New Catholic World*, 223(1980), pp. 205-208.

This article sees the good leader as an enabler who empowers others and releases a potential in the follower. The biblical concept of leadership is found in service. Life as a ransom (Mt 20:28) means release, releasing the full potential in the followers. Trust and listening are prerequisites. Leaders are challenged to be available, accountable and vulnerable (in the sense of the risk involved in an imperfect world), have vision, values, and communication skills. However, the source of true leadership is rooted in simplicity. The article highlights many significant dimensions of leadership that are readily applicable to existential situations.

Chambers, Thomas E. CSC. "The Spiritual Dimension of Christ Centered Leadership." *Today's Catholic Teacher*, 14(1981), p. 26.

The article emphasizes Christ as focus and foundation of religious leadership. Qualities of generosity, forgiveness and compassion are identified as well as the ability to tolerate the hurts of being misunderstood, misquoted and misinterpreted.

_____"The Spirit to Lead." *Today's Catholic Teacher*, 14 (1981), p. 28.

According to the author leadership with a spiritual orientation can be learned, developed and cultivated. The prerequisites are maturity and unlimited confidence. The importance of well defined goals for the leader is emphasized. Other qualities include communication, expectations for self and for the group, alertness, awareness and consciousness.

Connolly, K. "Adult Education." *New Catholic World*, 223 (1980), pp. 238-239.

The author uses the articles in the current issue of the periodical to stimulate group discussion on the various topics. The format and questions are easily followed and can be utilized by a variety of groups.

Cunningham, Agnes. "Pastoral Leadership in the Early Church." *Chicago Studies*, 17(1978), pp. 357-370.

The focus is on pastoral leadership in the patristic era. Who were the pastors? What were the major pastoral concerns? How did they exercise ministry in light of their concerns? To what extent did the exercise of their ministry as leaders in the church contribute to the development of other ministries in the early Christian community? These interesting questions are addressed in terms of Clement, Iraneas, Cyprian and Ignatius. The awareness of Christian dignity, views of the church and the life of faith are examined in terms of Ignatius. Some implications for today are presented.

Dominian, Jack. "Authority and Paternalism." *Way*, 12 (1972), pp. 199-210.

Since the problems of authority affect every form of life, the author perceives the reasonableness of looking at the structure of the family for a clarification and understanding of the origin of authority in the human personality. There is a strong reliance on Freud and Erikson for understanding early human development. With this background church and authority is examined as well as the New Testament foundations. Aspects of the article would need to be rewritten in light of changes in family structures. The value is in identifying basic human needs as an underpinning for the exercise of leadership.

Doohan, Helen. "Contrasts in Prophetic Leadership: Isaiah and Jeremiah," *Biblical Theology Bulletin*, 13 (1983), pp. 39-43.

This article examines the classical prophets from the perspective of leadership. Isaiah and Jeremiah are studied in terms of their unique historical situations and their differing understandings of the covenant. The significant factors in the leadership of these two prophets are presented as well as some challenges for religious leaders today.

Edwards, P. "The Myth of Authority." *Way*, 12 (1972), pp. 179-189.

The personal, historical and existential reflections of the author are presented in this article.

Fenhagen, James C. *Mutual Ministry: New Vitality for the Local Church*. New York: The Seabury Press, 1977.

This very readable book focuses on the local church in terms of ministry and Christian discipleship. The author touches many dimensions of responsible Christian life in today's world. The implications for religious leadership are both implicit and explicit.

Freemesser, George. "Spiritual Leadership." *Studies in Formative Spirituality*, 3(1982), pp. 25-39.

In this article the exploration of a "being there" or loving presence model for leadership is presented after examples of "woundedness" are examined. The tendency to focus on exterior concerns rather than interior life as exemplified in excessive activity, is seen as an aberration of responsibility. The maladies of our era are identified as the loss of inner peace and acceptance of self. Furthermore, aggression, misdirected spiritual energy, and loss of meaning are other diseases of society. While the author utilizes his own background and experience in presenting the situation, a positive portrayal of encountering Jesus as the spiritual leader is also presented. The value of the article is in highlighting the needs for spiritual leadership in committed people.

Futrell, John Carroll, SJ. "The Future of Religious Life: Challenge to Leadership and Formation." *Human Development*, 2(1981), pp. 6-17.

The article offers a brief overview of the last three decades in terms of religious life. The signs of the times in our secular culture are explored in an overview as changes in government, technology, and a growing narcissism. Religious life is influenced by the culture and this affects the view a person has of himself/herself as well as their understanding of religious life. Speculations about the future include a deepened life of faith and prayer, a profoundly shared experience in community and ministry and a shared understanding of religious life and vows in the church. The religious leader is called upon to hold three profound operational attitudes in creative tension: peace, patience, passion. The challenge to leadership is generally implicit throughout the article.

Gangel, Kenneth O. "Spirituality and Leadership." *Studies in Formative Spirituality*, 3 (1982), pp. 41-52.

In this article a balanced approach to ministry and prayer is shown to have scriptural foundations. The New Testament roots of spirituality are examined. A Christian spirituality based on a spirituality of gift is seen as a result of the scriptural insights. Ultimately the leadership person must model the person Jesus. Spiritual leadership as meekness, membership and ministry, is also touched upon by the author. The article seems more of a highlighting rather than a synthesizing of ideas.

Gill, James J., SJ. "The Stresses of Leadership." *Human Development*, 1(1980), pp. 17-25.

The article deals with stress and its positive and negative aspects termed eustress and distress. How is stress related to leadership? The author suggests that it revolves around the change, movement and development, which often arouses conflict. The signs of stress in self and in others are very helpful and these include mental and physical signs. Leader — follower relationships are examined and ways of dealing with stress are offered. The article is both insightful and practical.

Gottemoeller, Doris, RSM. "Women and Leadership in the Church: Problems and Promise." *New Catholic World*, 223 (1980), pp. 201-204.

Leadership as a facility in affecting change in structures, attitudes and beliefs, and as influencing the corporate other is described and discussed. Some leaders create their own forums and thereby exercise leadership. Is this diversity possible in the church? The author purports that the church must expand its concept of change and development if creative leadership will develop. Identifiable problems include clericalism, structural sexism, relationship between lay women and religious. Women are generally in support roles. Yet, a new leadership is on the horizon. The gifts of the Spirit are widely distributed in the community, and therefore, according to this author, there is no vocation crisis.

Greenleaf, Robert K. *Servant Leadership: A Journey into the Nature of Legitimate Power and Greatness.* New York: Paulist Press, 1977.

An excellent book on the subject of leadership. The author deals with such topics as, the servant as leader, the institution as servant, servant leadership in the churches, all of which are readily applicable to an understanding of religious leadership. However, institutional, educational and business dimensions are also examined in terms of servant leadership. This breadth and depth treatment of the subject is a fine perspective from which to develop a fuller understanding from a religious focal point.

_____ "The Leadership Crisis — What is is and what to do about it: A Personal View." *Humanitas*, 14 (1978), pp. 297-308.

The neglect of preparation for and development of leadership is attributed to the universities and the author challenges universities to create new dreams. The vision and the nuturing of new leadership will come from the saving remnant; the minority and the few faculty who have a clear sense of how institutions can change, will lead by persuasion. The persuasive atmosphere of the dream itself will lead to a response that will regenerate the university. The article also examines power in its coercive, manipulative and persuasive forms. Power as persuasion is dealt with in an insightful manner. The article is not only interesting and challenging but it is easily related to the crisis in religious leadership.

_____ "Spirituality as Leadership." *Studies in Formative Spirituality*, 3 (1982), pp. 53-64.

An autobiographical introduction sets the stage for an article which is thought provoking and challenging. What does it mean to lead? What is spirit and spiritual? What are the failures in religious leadership? The issues of power, money and competition are related to spirituality as leadership. Monasteries and seminaries are asked to infuse spiritual vitality into the churches. Why are these institutions failing? For the author, the prime formative challenge of our times is the nurturing of servants in all areas of life.

Hall, Brian P., Helen Thompson. *Leadership Through Values.* New York: Paulist Press, 1980.

This is a very fine book with some significant insights on the developmental aspects of leadership. The seven levels of leadership within the phases of consciousness and the stages of value development are presented in chart and narrative form. The skills necessary to each stage of leadership development are presented. The value of the presentation is not only in a studied assessment of leadership, but also in some possible directions for the development of leadership in church and society.

Hamachek, Don E. "Dynamics of Self: Other Perceptions and their Relationship to Leadership Style." *Humanitas* 14 (1978), pp. 355-366.

The article focuses on an examination of three questions regarding self-perception and leadership. Self-esteem, self-acceptance and self-awareness are the identifiable components of successful leadership. A contrasting leadership style is also presented which results from different self-other perceptions. The article is a very fine well documented analysis demonstrating the positive and negative effects of a good or poor self-esteem in leaders.

Harvanek, Robert. "The Expectations of Leadership." *Way*, 15(1975), pp. 20-33.

This excellent article on leadership begins by reflecting on the ambiguity of the contemporary need for leadership, not a leader. Contemporary understandings of leadership are explored and some insights from the business world are presented. In the business community which has its own authority structures, leadership is measured by success and results. The author also looks at the community which can prefer one or another type of leader. In examining the community dimensions of leadership, three stages in community life are developed: 1. the situation of coming into existence, 2. the existence of peace and prosperity, 3. a crisis which threatens its existence from within or without. Each stage demands a unique kind of leadership. The church is identified as being in a time of crisis with its consequent demands on leadership persons. In addition, the ecclesiology or models of church, out of which the leaders operate, affect leadership style. Finally, the level of human development in the followers affects the kind of leadership which will be demanded or allowed. Leadership traits, therefore, include strength and a response to the felt needs of community with a sense of timing and a sense of future.

Hennessey, James, SJ. "John Carroll, American Bishop." *New Catholic World*, 223(1980), pp. 225-227.

In this article a religious leader is presented by the author. John Carroll was a man of his times, and his style of being a bishop has rarely been matched. It combined a sympathetic awareness for the contemporary scene with a rich knowledge of the church's past and its theological thinking. Bishop Carroll's understanding of ecclesiastical leadership and highlights of his approach to ministry provide some interesting insights into a religious leader of the 18th century.

Hoeing, Therese. "The Necessity of Weakness for Christian Leadership." *Review for Religious* 39(1980), pp. 18-21.

The author proposes weakness as a necessary quality for leadership in the Christian community. Weakness is described as an awareness of personal imperfection which confronts the gamut of human brokenness, pain, and sin. Weakness describes a condition of equality with those to whom we minister and an attitude of surrender to God. It is the power of God that transforms. The article offers a needed perspective for the understanding of religious leadership.

Hogan, William F. "Leadership in Weakness." *Studies in Formative Spirituality*, 3 (1982), pp. 65-74.

The author examines the situation in which people shrink from religious or spiritual leadership. He reflects that Christian spirituality has not taken into account the positive aspects and the real blessing of human weakness. The dimensions of human weakness and powerlessness are presented. However, persons are wisely admonished not to hide behind weakness in order to avoid responding to calls for spiritual help in prayer and direction. The article is a well integrated approach to the topic.

Hollander, Edwin P. "What is the Crisis of Leadership?" *Humanitas*, 14 (1970), pp. 285-296.

Leadership is described as a process which depends very much on the relationship between leaders and followers. In retrospect, leadership was explained by the "great man" theory, "trait approach," "situational approach," "contingency models," "transactional approach." The movement now is towards an appreciation of mutual influence between leader and follower. Leadership as a transaction is explored in reasonable depth, as well as the concepts of legitimacy and authority. A good distinction is made between leadership and headship. Credibility and accountability are briefly examined in terms of the Carter presidency. While the focus of the article is broader than religious leadership, it is readily applicable to organizational leadership in the church.

Kelly, Eileen, Sister, SSA. "Learning Through Leadership: Interview." *Human Development*, 1 (1980), pp. 6-13.

An interview is conducted with a successful superior of a religious community who is going out of office. Leadership in community, the changes in religious life and leadership qualities are discussed.

MacCormack, John R. "Leadership as Shared Conscience." *Humanitas,* 14 (1978), pp. 321-332.

The article presents a historical overview of leadership in terms of individualistic and collectivist approaches. Distinctions are made between leaders and terrorist power. The unique contribution of the Hebrews is discussed, for in this culture, God is the ruler. The principles and approaches of well known leaders are presented. Moral values, politics, brotherhood, justice, love, freedom, are the principal values of various historical and/or religious leaders. The positive and negative dimensions of leadership are also presented. Finally, leadership and freedom are related in terms of shared conscience. The author's conclusions are based on historical evidence.

Maloney, George A. "The Elder of the Christian East as Spiritual Leader."*Studies in Formative Spirituality* 3 (1982), pp. 75-87.

In this article the anima attitude or the diffused awareness in the Eastern approach to spiritual leadership is characterized in the elder or guru. Charismatic leadership and spiritual fatherhood are addressed historically and existentially. The characteristics or qualities of the spiritual father are loving friendship relationship and a duty to love, discern, pray for the directee. Listening, humility, and above all, love are emphasized by the author. The article can complement other insights into religious leadership.

McKay, Mary. "Some Obstacles to Authentic Leadership." *Humanitas* 14 (1978), pp. 333-354.

The underlying assumption of the author is that leadership is both dynamic and situational. The attitudes or actions which obstruct an individual's becoming a leader are perceptual predispositions, motivations, an authoritarian attitude with roots in a deficient sense of self, a lack of tolerance for ambiguity residing in a need for a well-order manageable world, flight from responsibility because of fear of one's greatness and fear of becoming one's better self, and distortions of expression. The well documented article relies on experts in psychology and sociology for a fine beginning synthesis of the topic.

McNulty, Frank. "The Tensions of Leadership: The Priest." *New Catholic World*, 223 (1978), pp. 228-231.

Ten areas of tension are examined and very concrete examples are given in regard to priestly ministry and leadership. The dicotomy between dream and reality, prayer and action, blueprint ecclesiology and erector ecclesiology, care of self and care of others, distance and closeness, authority and freedom, are some of the sources of tension. The areas of tension can be applied to all involved in religious leadership whether they be priests, laity or religious.

Meissner, W. "Blind Guides." *Way*, 15 (1975), pp.3-10.

The author pursues a broader notion of authority in terms of relationship and a basic notion of Christian leadership in terms of service not power. The consequences of power and powerlessness/worthlessness are examined. Some of the major problems of lack of self-esteem and depression in religious personnel are seen as the result of worthlessness, a corollary of powerlessness. Freedom, initiative, capacity for responsible action are advocated for authentic life and spiritual vitality.

Moloney, Francis J. *Disciples and Prophets: A Biblical Model for The Religious Life*. New York: Crossroad, 1981.

The author identifies a biblical model for religious life within the context of the universal call to holiness. This foundation and the analysis and reinterpretation of well known biblical "proof texts" for the religious life, provide a solid basis for the exercise of contemporary leadership within religious communities.

Murphy-O'Connor, Jerome. *What is Religious Life? A Critical Reappraisal.* Wilmington: Michael Glazier, Inc., 1977.

This interesting book offers insight into the understanding of authority, and community within the context of religious life. A series of responses to the author's thesis comprise the second half of the book. This section sharpens the issues for the reader and offers further challenges to leaders and members of religious communities.

Murray, Noreen. "The Art of Religious Leadership." *Review for Religious*, 35 (1976), pp. 29-32.

The article presents an overview of religious leadership as seen in a religious superior or coordinator of a community. The author's reflection and synthesis highlight some necessary qualities and attitudes for religious leaders.

Myers, J. Gordon, SJ., Richard A. Schoenherr, Ph.D. "The Baptism of Power: Shared Decision Making in the Church." *New Catholic World*, 223 (1980), pp. 217-221.

The focus of the article is the diocese and an interesting assessment of power, influence and the concerns of the diocese is offered. Advisory councils as a leadership model in the church are presented. However, the present reality of little shared responsibility is also realistically portrayed. The ideal of shared decision making will need creative planning and education to become the new reality.

Neuman, Matthias, OSB., Jesse Nash. "Authority, Obedience and Personal Initiative in a Pluralistic Church." *Spirituality Today*, 32 (1980), pp. 218-236.

Part I. The goal of the article is to offer an integrated and wholistic approach to authentic Christian discipleship. The various aspects and implications of pluralism are presented in the context of society and church life. A weakening of structures, a view of community as dynamic and changing, a priority of building responsible life styles over institutional church affiliation, are presented as conclusions of the phenomenon of pluralism. Pluralism now challenges authority in the Catholic Church in crises proportions. Pre-Vatican II positions are briefly presented as well as a new understanding of authority. Pluralism is challenging traditional views, while a supporting style of leadership is becoming a necessity for vibrant personal and social growth. Obedience, which is found in a community searching for the truth, is the desired end in the new approach. This article is very good in describing the present situation, recent shifts and their implications.

Part II. The focus turns to personal initiative which is seen as a possible link between authority and obedience in a pluralistic church. The author presents the foundations for personal initiative and its implications for church in terms of interaction with culture, effect on ministry, authority and obedience.

Newton, Robert R. "Lay Leadership in Catholic Schools, Dimensions and Dilemmas." *New Catholic World*, 224 (1981), pp. 65-69.

In this paper presented to the Annual Convention of Chief Administrators of Catholic Education in October 1979, three dimensions of lay leadership are discussed: the ministry of teaching, the laity and policy making, lay leadership and the building of community. In regard to teaching, laity receive a direct call, not through a religious community. In previous times laity have not been responsible for the church's mission in education. Today, school boards with lay participation are a step forward, but care must be taken to maintain the Christian purpose of education. The communal dimensions of Catholic schools are attributed to homogeneity and transference. However, in a time of transition and change, the lay leadership will be called upon to solve many problems. Two major problems emerge when leadership is transferred to the laity: the revitalization of schools through a regular turnover of leadership and the development of programs which will develop competencies. Laity have less flexibility and financial resources to move and/or participate in the endeavor according to the author. These obstacles must be overcome in creative ways. Some interesting questions and issues are raised in the article.

O'Grady, John F. "Jesus: His Authority, Power and, Leadership." *Studies in Formative Spirituality*, 3 (1982), pp. 89-97.

The author sees the history of humankind demonstrating four kinds of authority: mystical, bureaucratic, learned and charismatic. The authority of Jesus is presented as charismatic for Jesus leads by the power of persuasion, offering inspiration as a leader. He also encourages others to use their talents, teaches, offers a goal in life, the means to attain the goal and forgives. The characteristics of an effective leader are seen in these qualities. Persuasion and inspiration are particularly necessary today.

Padovano, Anthony T. "Leadership and Authority." *New Catholic World*, 223(1980, pp.222-224.

This article considers the nature of authority, authority and jurisdiction, and the character of leadership in terms of the church. Clear descriptions of the issues and terms are presented and a dynamic portrayal of leadership and its relationship to the community are offered. The article is excellent in its clarity, readability, and challenge to rethink the leadership and authority issue within the church.

Pasquier, Jacques. "The Psychology of Leadership." *Way*, 15 (1975), pp. 34-45.

This excellent article addresses the issue of leader versus leadership. Various models of leadership are examined, including the political and the management model. Two main functions of leadership are identified as helping the group achieve its goals and helping the individual satisfy his/her needs. A person is a leader in so far as personal qualities are perceived by the group as the best means by which it can reach its goals and fulfill its needs. The real challenge of any group is to place leaders in situations where they can function as leaders, since leadership is effective in the social situation. Some very fine insights are offered on the level of community development and leadership. The author assumes that primary and secondary groups have different needs. Finally, spiritual leadership is presented as the only viable form of leadership in a Christian community. This leadership is the responsibility of the community and it involves an awareness of call, the ministry of healing and compassion, a challenge to a quality response to the gospel.

Perkins, Pheme. "Paul, Peter and the Shape of Early Christian Leadership." *New Catholic World*, 223 (1980), pp. 213-216.

In this article an overview of Paul, the apostle of weakness and Peter, the rock of the Christian community is presented. The Gospels, Letters and Acts form the basis of the author's observations.

Putrow, Mary Lou, Sister. "The Ministry of Leadership." *Sisters Today*, 48 (1976), pp. 97-103.

This article stimulates thinking and leads to an understanding of leadership by reflecting on personal experience and examining the expectations of leadership. Leadership as ministry is identified as flowing from a relationship with God to other persons, within the realities of the world situation. Good insights are incorporated into an understanding of leadership and some future perspectives are offered.

Rule, Philip. "Prophecy and Hierarchy." *Way*, 12 (1972), pp. 190-198.

The author presents institutional leadership and prophecy as a form of charismatic leadership in a futureshock society. Hierarchy and prophecy are seen as two healthy polarities which are reflected in the polarization of leadership. A future orientation is seen as essential to true renewal. The tension between institutional and charismatic leaders often guarantees that this perspective endures. The role of the prophet can foster the development of the vision and offer hope which is essential to real growth.

Ryan, Herbert J. "The Listening Leader." *Catholic Mind*, 78 (1980), pp. 26-35.

In this keynote address for the First National Convocation of Christian Leaders held at Stanford in August, 1979, Christian leadership and ministry are firmly grounded in Jesus. Both leadership and ministry demand fidelity and prayer. Paul and Jerome are used as examples of "listening leaders." The author advocates a de-emphasis on success and a concentration on commitment.

Sheets, J. "Whom Shall We Follow." *Way*, 15(1975), pp. 46-55.

The article initially treats pluralism in terms of diversity and division. Pluralism is not seen as new for conflicting claims in following authentic teaching is seen in the New Testament itself. The problem of leadership and authority in the apostolic church is addressed in the letters and the gospel of John. The article is strong in scriptural documentation. The answer to the question of whom to follow resides in the church itself, which upholds the truth.

Sollom, Wilfred. "The Technological Revolution." *Tablet*, 234 (1980), pp. 529-532.

According to the author the situation today challenges persons to spiritual leadership, or the ability to see spiritual significance in daily life. The article was an address to Association of Teaching Religious at Exeter University. Some foundations of spiritual leadership and a religious view of the world are presented in order to perceive technology in a Christian context.

Stanley, David. "Idealism and Realism in Paul." *Way*, 21 (1981), pp. 34-46.

The article, whose subtitle is "Liberation Christology and Christian Leadership", is a fine synthesis of Paul from this perspective. True leadership is perceived as freeing the group, liberating it into the fulness of its potential as persons and as a group. Paul is assessed as a spiritual leader in terms of his letters. The dynamic and situational dimensions of leadership are presented implicitly in the analysis.

Sullivan Francis Patrick, SJ."Authority's Icon: Brother/ Sister/ Jesus." *New Catholic World,* 223 (1980), pp. 209-212.

The author suggests that within the contemporary life span, authority has degenerated into power, and knowledge and love into ignorance within religion. However, a regeneration has also taken place. The regeneration proceeds from a recognition that religion is an act of spiritual creation not submission. The article emphasizes relationships, imagination, integration, and an aesthetic experience of revelation in furthering an understanding of authority.

Tetlow, Joseph A., SJ. "An Agenda for Leadership." *New Catholic World*, 222 (1979), pp. 12-15.

In this article, new dimensions of leadership are seen in team ministry, a new concept of parish, the relinquishing church models that are class based, the changes in the selection of leaders, and in an emphasis on justice and peace. The emergence of leadership in the American church is seen as a positive sign which the author reflects upon and identifies.

_____ "The Second Half-Generation."*New Catholic World*, 223 (1980), pp. 196-200.

Some interesting and challenging questions are put forth in this article which assessing the church's progress since Vatican II. Models of the church call forth certain kinds of leadership and followership while the stereotyping of organizations in a negative light can make leadership nearly impossible. Clarity, consultation, participation, shared responsibility and team work are needed. Authority is perceived in a new light and creates new burdens for the membership. Authority in certain movements and groups derives its identity from personal spiritual experience. According to the author, an awareness of spirituality and spiritual needs is seen as an essential dimension for the exercise of authority. The understanding of church as People of God, Mystical Body, Sacrament and Servant of the World, offers creative challenges to new leadership in the church.

Trigg, Joseph W. "The Charismatic Intellectual: Origen's Understanding of Religious Leadership". *Church History*, 50 (1981), pp. 5-19.

The article points out Origen's reliance on the Old Testament priesthood and Paul's understanding of charisma in order to understand developments in the early church. Priest and apostle are the symbols for religious authority chosen by Origen. Origen reconciles the roles of being an intellectual and a churchman through a coherent theory of religious leadership, a theory in which churchmanship becomes a function of intellectual achievement. The implications of the charismatic intellectual are explored in an interesting and insightful presentation.

Overman, C. "Building Followership." *Sisters Today*, 50(1979), pp. 623-627.

The author closely identifies leadership and followership. Although leaders have the primary role in building follower-ship, the aware response of the members is an indispensable factor. Building blocks to followership include interdependence, credibility, legitimacy, persuasion and motivation. Mutual responsibility is demonstrated in regard to each factor presented in this succent and practical article.

Volleberg, J.J.A. "Religious Leadership" in *Minister? Pastor? Prophet?* Lucas Grollenberg, et al. New York: Crossroads, 1981, pp. 41-56.

The question of leadership versus religious leadership is addressed by the author as well as the ecclesiology which affects leadership style. Leadership functions in a situation of tension, while integrated leadership skillfully combines autonomous leadership with the activity of the group. This ability is important if the gifts of persons are to be fully utilized in the church. A distribution of leadership roles is advocated and collegiality as a principle of leadership is addressed.

Walsh, J. "By What Authority." *Way*, 12 (1972), pp. 175-178.

This overview article speaks to the connection between authority and faith. Within the Christian context, an understanding of Christ and a living out of the implications of that relationship is essential.

Wright, J. "Led by the Spirit." *Way*, 15 (1975), pp. 11-19.

The author suggests that the perspective on leadership in the Christian community is that of leadership as the gift and work of the Spirit. The scriptural basis of this understanding is then presented. Two important dimensions of leadership are a focus on goals and on the community. Among the more important qualities of leadership are ability to communicate, dedication and commitment, loving service, personal concern, encouragement and the ability to inspire confidence. The article is a fine treatment of the subject.

# BIBLIOGRAPHY

Abbott, Walter, ed. *The Documents of Vatican II.* New York: Guild Press, 1966.

Bailey, J. A. "Who wrote II Thessalonains?" *NTS* 25 (1978-79), pp. 131-145.

Banks, Robert. *Paul's Idea of Community, The Early House Churches in the Historical Setting.* Grand Rapids, Michigan: Wm. B. Eerdmans Publishing Co., 1980.

Barrett, C. K. *The Epistle to the Romans.* London: Adam and Charles Black, 1962.

_____*The First Epistle to the Corinthians.* 2nd. ed. London: Adam and Charles Black, 1971.

_____ *The Second Epistle to the Corinthians.* New York: Harper and Row Publishers, 1973.

Beare, F.W. *A Commentary of the Epistle to the Philippians.* 2nd. ed. London: Adam and Charles Black, 1969.

Bernhard, Leopold W. "Authority in Decline." *Dialog,* 20 (1981), pp. 200-204.

Best, Ernest. *The First and Second Epistles to the Thessalonians.* London: Adam and Charles Black, 1972.

Betz, Hans Dieter. *Galatians: A Commentary on Paul's Letter to the Churches in Galatia.* Philadelphia: Fortress Press, 1979.

Bornkamm, Gunther. *Paul.* New York: Harper and Row Publishers, 1969.

_____ "The Letter to the Romans as Paul's Last Will and Testament." In *The Romans Debate.* K. P. Donfried, ed. pp. 17-31.

Bright, John. *Jeremiah.* Garden City, New York: Doubleday, Inc., 1965.

_____ *A History of Israel.* 2nd. ed. London: SCM Press, 1972.

Brinsmead, Bernard Hungerford. *Galatians — Dialogical Response to Opponents.* JBL Dissertation Series 65. Chico, CA.: Scholars Press, 1982.

Bruce, F.F. *The Letters of Paul. An Expanded Paraphrase.* Grand Rapids: William B. Eerdmans Publishing Co., 1965.

Burns, James MacGregor. *Leadership.* New York: Harper Colophon Books, 1979.

Buttrick, George Arthur, ed. *The Interpreter's Dictionary of the Bible.* New York: Abingdon Press, 1962.

Caird, G. B. *Paul's Letters From Prison.* Oxford: University Press, 1976.

Campbell, W. S. "The Romans Debate." *Journal for the Study of the New Testament,* 10 (1981) pp. 19-28.

_____ "Romans III as a Key to the Structure and Thought of the Letter." *NT,* 23 (1981) pp. 22-40.

Clements, Ronald Ernest. *Isaiah 1-39.* Grand Rapids: William B. Eerdmans Publishing Co., 1980.

Conzelmann, Hans. *1 Corinthians.* Philadelphia: Fortress Press, 1975.

Cranfield, C. E. B. *A Critical and Exegetical Commentary on the Epistle to the Romans.* Vols. I and II. Edinburgh: T. and T. Clark Ltd. 1975 and 1979.

Davies, W. D. *Paul and Rabbinic Judaism*. London: SPCK, 1965.

_____ "Paul and the People Israel." *NTS*, 24 (1977-78), pp. 4-39.

Dodd, C. H. *The Epistle of Paul to the Romans*. 1932; rpt. London: Collins, Fontana Books, 1959.

Donfried, Karl Paul, ed. *The Romans Debate*. Minneapolis: Augsburg Press, 1977.

Doohan, Helen. "Burnout: A Critical Issue for the 1980's." *Journal of Religion and Health*, 21 (1982), pp. 352-358.

_____ "Isaiah and Jeremiah: Contrasts in Prophetic Leadership." *BTB*, 13 (1983), pp. 39-43.

Doohan, Leonard. "Contemporary Theologies of the Laity: an overview since Vatican II." *Communio*, 7 (1980), pp. 225-242.

_____ "The Spiritual Value of Leisure." *Spirituality Today*, 31 (1981), pp. 157-167.

Eckman, Barbara. "A Quantitative Metrical Alalysis of the Philippian Hymn." *NTS*, 26 (1979-80), pp. 258-266.

Ellis, E. Earle. "Paul and his Co-Workers." *NTS*, 17 (1970-71), pp. 437-452.

Fallon, Francis T. *2 Corinthians*. Wilmington Delaware: Michael Glazier, 1980.

Finley, Mitchel B. "The Spirit of Kenosis: A Principle of Pauline Spirituality." In *A Companion to Paul*, M.J. Taylor, ed. New York: Alba House, 1975, pp. 157-164.

Fitzmyer, Joseph A. "The Letter to the Philippians." *JBC*, pp. 247-253.

_____ "The Letter to the Romans" pp. 291-331.

_____ *Pauline Theology: a Brief Sketch*. New Jersey: Prentice Hall, Inc., 1977.

_____"The Gospel in the Theology of Paul." *Interpretation*, 33 (1979), pp. 339-350.

_____ Review of *Redating the New Testament*, by John A.T. Robinson, *Interpretation*, 32 (1978), pp. 309-313.

Freyne, Sean. *The World of The New Testament*. Wilmington, Delaware: Michael Glazier Inc., 1980.

Gager, J. *Kingdom and Community. The Social World of Early Christianity*. Englewood Cliffs: Prentice Hall, 1975.

Grant, R. *A Historical Introduction to the New Testament*. London: Collins, 1971.

Grayston, Kenneth. *The Letters of Paul to the Philippians and to the Thessalonians*. Cambridge: University Press, 1967.

Greehy, John J. "Philippians." In *A New Catholic Commentary on Holy Scripture*. Fuller, et al.,eds.pp.1192-1197.

Greenleaf, Robert K. *Servant Leadership: A Journey into the Nature of Legitimate Power and Greatness*. New York: Paulist Press, 1977.

Grollenberg, Lucas et al. *Minister? Pastor? Prophet? Grassroots Leadership in the Churches*. New York: Crossroad, 1981.

Gross, Bertram M. *The Managing of Organizations* Vols. I and II. New York: The Free Press of Glencoe, 1964.

Guthrie, Donald. *Galatians*. London: Oliphants, 1969.

Hall, Brian P., and Helen Thompson. *Leadership Through Values*. New York: Paulist Press, 1980.

Hamachek, Don E. "Dynamics of Self-Other Perceptions and Their Relationship to Leadership Style." *Humanitas*, 14 (1978), pp. 355-366.

Haring, Bernard. *Theology of Protest.* New York: Farrar, Straus and Giroux, 1970.

Hengel, Martin. *Judaism and Hellenism.* Philadelphia: Fortress Press, 1980.

_____ *Acts and the History of the Earliest Christianity.* Philadelphia: Fortress Press, 1980.

Hersey, Paul, and Ken Blanchard. *Management of Organizational Behavior.* 4th ed. New Jersey: Prentice Hall, 1982.

Heschel, Abraham J. *The Prophets.* New York: Harper and Row, Publishers, 1962.

Hock, Ronald. "The Workshop as a Social Setting for Paul's Missionary Preaching." *CBQ* 41 (1979), pp.438-450.

Hollander, Edwin P. "What is the Crisis of Leadership?" *Humanitas*, 14 (1970), pp. 285-296.

Holmberg, Bengt. *Paul and Power: The Structure of Authority in the Primitive Church as Reflected in the Pauline Epistles.* Philadelphia: Fortress Press, 1980.

Howard, George. "Phil 2:6-11 and the Human Christ." *CBQ*, 40 (1978), pp. 368-387.

Hurd, J. C. *The Origin of First Corinthians.* London: SPCK, 1965.

Jervell, Jacob. "The Letter to Jerusalem." In *The Roman Debate.* K. P. Donfried, ed. pp. 61-74.

Jewett, Robert. "Major Impulses in the Theological Interpretation of Romans since Barth." *Interpretation*, 34 (1980), pp. 17-31.

_____ "Romans as an Ambassadorial Letter." *Interpretation*, 36 (1982), pp. 5-20.

Johnson, Luke T. *Decision Making in the Church.* Philadelphia: Fortress Press, 1983.

Karris, Robert J. "The Occasion of Romans: A Response to Prof. Donfreid." In *The Roman Debate*. Donfried, ed. pp. 149-151.

Koester, H. "The Letter to the Philippians." *IDB*, Supplementary Volume, pp. 665-666.

Kummel, Werner George. *Introduction to the New Testament*. London: SCM Press, 1965.

Lightfoot, J. B. *The Epistle of St. Paul to the Galatians*. 1865; rpt. Grand Rapids: The Zondervan Publishing House, 1957.

Lindblom, Johannes. *Prophecy in Ancient Israel*. Philadelphia: Fortress Press, 1962.

Maccoby, Michael. *The Leader: A New Face for American Management*. New York: Simon and Schuster, 1981.

Malina, Bruce J. *The New Testament World*. Atlanta: John Knox Press, 1981.

Mann, Frederic. "Philippians 2:6-11: A Judeo-Christian hymn." *TD*, 26 (1978), pp. 4-10.

Martin, Ralph P. *Philippians*. London: Oliphants, 1976.

McKenzie, John L. *Authority in the Church*. New York: Sheed and Ward, 1966.

Meagher, John C. *The Way of the Word: The Beginning and The Establishing of Christian Understanding*. New York: Seabury Press, 1975.

Mearns, C. L. "Early Eschatological Development in Paul: The Evidence of I and II Thess." *NTS*, 27 (1980-81), pp. 137-157.

Meeks, Wayne A. *The First Urban Christians: The Social World of the Apostle Paul*. New Haven: Yale University Press, 1983.

Montague, George T. *The Living Thought of Saint Paul.* Benzinger, 1976.

Moore, A. L. *1 and 2 Thessalonians.* London: Nelson, 1969.

Morgan, Florence. *United to a death like Christ's: Rom 6:5a.* Unpublished diss. Katholieke Universiteit Leuven, 1982.

Munck, Johannes. *Paul and the Salvation of Mankind.* Richmond, Va.: John Knox Press, 1959.

_____ "1 Thess 1:9-10 and the Missionary Preaching of Paul. Textual Exegesis and Hermeneutic Reflections." *NTS,* 9 (1962-63), pp. 95-110.

Munro, Winsome. *Authority in Peter and Paul.* New York: Cambridge University Press, 1983.

Murphy-O'Connor, Jerome. "Christological Anthropology in Phil. II, 6-11." *RB,* 83 (1976), pp. 25-50.

_____ "Eucharist and Community in First Corinthians *Worship,* 50 (1976), pp. 370-385; 51 (1976), pp. 56-69.

_____ "Freedom or the Ghetto (1 Cor 8:1-13; 10:23 -11:1)." *RB,* 85 (1978), pp. 543-574.

_____ "Corinthian Slogans in 1 Cor 6:12-20." *CBQ,* 40 (1978), pp. 391-396.

_____ *1 Corinthians.* Wilmington, Delaware: Michael Glazier, Inc., 1979.

_____ "Sex and Logic in 1 Corinthians 11, 2-16." *CBQ* 42 (1980), pp. 482-500.

_____ *St. Paul's Corinth.* Text and Archaeology. Wilmington, Delaware: Michael Glazier Inc., 1983.

O'Neill, J. C. *Paul's Letter to the Romans.* Baltimore: Penguin Books, 1975.

Padovano, Anthony T. "Leadership and Authority." *N. C. World,* 223 (1980), pp. 222-224.

Parvey, Constance. "The Theology and Leadership of Women in the New Testament." In *Religion and Sexism.* Rosemary Radford Ruether, ed. New York: Simon and Schuster, 1974.

Pasquier, J. "The Psychology of Leadership." *Way,* 15 (1975), pp. 34-45.

Perkins, Pheme. *Ministering in The Pauline Churches.* New York: Paulist Press, 1982.

Perrin, Norman. *The New Testament: An Introduction.* New York: Harcourt, Brace and Jovanovich, Inc., 1974.

Plevnik, Joseph. "1 Thess 5, 1-11: Its Authenticity, Intention and Message." *Biblica,* 60 (1979), pp. 71-90.

Putrow, Mary Lou. "The Ministry of Leadership." *Sisters Today,* 48 (1976), pp. 97-103.

Ramsay, William M. *A Historical Commentary on St. Paul's Epistle to the Galatians.* 1898; rpt. Grand Rapids: Baker Book Co., 1965.

Reese, James M. *1 and 2 Thessalonians.* Wilmington, Delaware: Michael Glazier, Inc., 1979.

Ridderbos, Herman. *Paul: An Outline of His Theology.* Grand Rapids: William B. Eerdmans Publishing Co., 1975.

Roetzel, Calvin. *The Letters of Paul: Conversations in Context.* 2nd. ed. Atlanta: John Knox Press, 1982.

Ruether, Rosemary Radford, ed. *Religion and Sexism; Images of Woman in the Jewish and Christian Traditions* New York: Simon and Schuster, 1974.

Sanders, E. P. *Paul and Palestinian Judaism.* Philadelphia: Fortress Press, 1977.

Schillebeeckx, Edward. *Ministry: Leadership in the Community of Jesus Christ.* New York: Crossroad, 1981.

Schnackenburg, Rudolph. "Community Cooperation in the New Testament." *Concilium*, 77 (1972), pp. 9-19.

Scott, R. B. Y. *The Relevance of the Prophets.* New York: Macmillan Publishing Co., Inc., 1944.

Schutz, John Howard. *Paul and the Anatomy of Apostolic Authority.* Cambridge: University Press, 1975.

Spicq, Ceslaus, *Agapé in the New Testament.* St. Louis: B. Herder Book Co., 1965.

Stanley, David M. *Christ's Resurrection in Pauline Soteriology.* Diss. Rome: Pontifical Biblical Institute, 1952.

_____ "Authority in the Church: A New Testament Reality." *CBQ*, 29 (1967), pp. 555-573.

_____ "Idealism and Realism in Paul." *Way*, 21 (1981) pp. 34-46.

Stendahl, Krister. *Paul Among Jews and Gentiles and Other Essays.* Philadelphia: Fortress Press, 1976.

Stogdill, Ralph M. *Handbook of Leadership.* New York: Free Press, 1974.

Taylor, Michael J., (ed) *A Companion to Paul.* New York: Alba House, 1975.

Theissen, Gerd. *The Social Setting of Pauline Christianity; Essays on Corinth.* Philadelphia: Fortress Press, 1982.

Thrall, Margaret E. *The First and Second Letters of Paul to the Corinthians.* Cambridge: University Press, 1965.

Trompf, G. W. "On Attitudes toward Women in Paul and Paulinist Literature: 1 Cor. 11. 3-6 and Its Context." *CBQ*, 42 (1980), pp. 196-215.

Volleberg, J. J. A. "Religious Leadership." *Minister? Pastor? Prophet?* Lucas Grollenberg, ed. New York: Crossroads, 1981, pp. 41-56.

Von Rad, Gerhard. *The Message of the Prophets.* New York: Harper and Row Publishers, 1967.

Whiteley, D. E. H. *The Theology of St. Paul.* Philadelphia: Fortress Press, 1964.

Williams, Sam K. "The Righteousness of God in Romans." *JBL*, 99 (1980), pp. 241-290.

Witherington, Ben. "Rite and Rights for Women — Galatians 3:28." *NTS*, 27 (1980-81), pp. 593-604.

Wright, J. "Led by the Spirit." *Way*, 15 (1975), pp. 11-19.

# INDEX OF AUTHORS

# INDEX OF SUBJECTS